# WOMEN'S BASKETBALL

## The Post Player's Handbook

Anne Donovan

Wish Publishing
Terre Haute, Indiana
www.wishpublishing.com

LCCN: 2001086540

Proofread by Heather Lowhorn
Cover designed by Phil Velikan
Cover photo by McGrath Photography

Printed in the United States of America
10 9 8 7 6 5 4 3 2 1

Published in the United States by
Wish Publishing
P.O. Box 10337
Terre Haute, IN 47801, USA
www.wishpublishing.com

Distributed in the United States by
Cardinal Publishers Group
7301 Georgetown Road, Suite 118
Indianapolis, Indiana 46268
www.cardinalpub.com

## Acknowledgments

I would like to extend special thanks to Dr. Rose Battaglia and Mariane Stanley. The strong coaching that I received from Coach Battaglia while at Paramus Catholic High School enabled me to enter college with solid fundamentals and a desire to be the best. At Old Dominion, Coach Stanley molded me into a national champion and an All-American.

I'd also like to thank Holly Kondras, Phil Velikan and Tom Doherty of Wish Publishing, as well as Dale Ratermann for editorial assistance.

## Publisher's Note

Anne Donovan, quite simply, was the most dominating post player in the history of women's basketball. She was inducted into the Naismith Basketball Hall of Fame in 1995 and was a member of three U.S. Olympic teams.

Anne is too modest to sing her own praises, but Wish Publishing is happy to do that for her. Following her successful playing career, Anne became a successful coach. We feel there is no one more qualified to instruct today's young aspiring post players or assist coaches developing those players.

Anne helped lead Old Dominion University to a 37-1 record and the AIAW national title as a freshman in 1980, then went on to lead ODU to an AIAW third place finish in 1981 and to the NCAA Final Four in 1983. In her four-year college playing career, Old Dominion compiled a 116-20 record (.853). She was named the Naismith and Champion Player of the Year in 1983 as well as an All-American in 1981, 1982 and 1983. She finished her playing career at ODU as the Lady Monarch's all-time leading scorer (2,179 points), rebounder (1,976) and shot blocker (801), and still owns 25 ODU records. In fact, her career blocks mark of 801 at Old Dominion easily exceeds the NCAA career record of 428 held by

Jenia Miller of Cal State Fullerton. (The NCAA did not begin officially keeping blocked shots until 1988.)

Anne was a member of the gold medal winning 1984 and 1988 U.S. Olympic basketball teams, as well as the 1980 Olympic team that boycotted the Moscow Games, making her one of only four male or female U.S. players to have been named to three U.S. Olympic basketball squads.

A member of a remarkable 12 USA Basketball teams and one of the most decorated players in USA Basketball history, she also played on the silver medal 1983 and gold medal 1986 World Championship teams, the 1983 and 1987 Pan American Games squads that earned golds, the silver medal winning 1981 World University Games team, as well as the gold medal 1978 and 1979 Olympic Festival East teams. All told, of a possible 11 medals, she captured nine golds and two silvers.

After college, Anne spent five seasons playing professionally in Shizuoka, Japan (1984-88), and one season in Modena, Italy (1989), before returning to Old Dominion as an assistant coach for six years (1990-95). With Anne on the coaching staff, ODU earned four Colonial Athletic Association (CAA) conference titles (1992, 1993, 1994, 1995), five NCAA Tournament berths and compiled a record of 115-62 (.650).

In 1995 Anne was named head coach at East Carolina University. In three seasons she helped turn around a program that posted only 10 wins in the previous two years before her arrival. In 1997 she led the Lady Pirates to the CAA tournament championship game for the first time since 1992.

Anne was named an assistant coach for the 1997 USA Basketball Women's World Championship Qualifying Team that posted a 4-2 record, earned the silver medal in Brazil and qualified the U.S. for the 13th World Championship. During its 13-game pre-competition exhibition tour of Canada, Germany and Slovakia, she helped lead the U.S. squad to an impressive 12-1 record and a pair of tournament titles.

Anne was named head coach of the professional Philadelphia Rage of the American Basketball League in May 1998. The league ceased operations in December 1998 after she guided the team to a 9-5 record. (The team was 13-31 the season before Anne's arrival.)

In 2001, after serving as the interim head coach of the Indiana Fever for one year, Anne became the head coach of the WNBA Charlotte Sting.

We at Wish Publishing are pleased that Anne has chosen us to publish her first book.

Holly Kondras
Wish Publishing

22
11

# Foreword

The game of basketball has changed through the years. While the three-point shot is an important aspect of the game, learning solid post play seems to be a rarity among today's young players.

As young players grow tall at an earlier age, a lot of those players are being taken away from the block and put outside where their height advantage might allow them to shoot uncontested three-pointers. Some coaches think that a big "3" is more advantageous than a good post player. It's not glamorous to fight for position at the low post, catch the ball and shoot a short shot. Post play, though, is still a very vital part of the women's game. Every coach should desire a good, strong post player who can score, rebound and defend.

The most decorated post player in women's basketball history was Anne Donovan. Anne's résumé as a basketball player may be unmatched in the world. She is a member of two halls of fame—the Women's Basketball Hall of Fame and the Naismith Hall of Fame. She played the game at the highest level and won at the highest level.

Anne did not become a dominating post player just because she was tall. She learned the fundamentals of the game early and worked hard. That allowed her to continue to grow as a player throughout her career. She received good coaching, and she played at a young age against older, more experienced international players. That competition allowed her game to develop even faster.

Since retiring as a player, Anne has become an excellent coach. She understands the game of basketball and understands players. She has great patience and a demeanor around players that brings immediate respect. If I were a post player — especially a young post player — I would want to learn from Anne. She has done it all, at every level the game offers.

This collection of drills and tips will help players of any age or skill level. It also will help coaches develop better post players. Read and study this book, then go to the gym and work. While other players are launching three-pointers, work on your footwork, boxing out and all the other fundamentals of post play. That's what will make you a better player and your team a better team.

Nell Fortner, Head Coach
U.S. Women's Basketball Team
2000 Summer Olympics

# Table of Contents

# Introduction

Post players are a dying breed today. It is a specialty that is needed at every level — high school, college and professionally. If a player is able to develop the necessary skills to become a good post player, there always will be a place on the team for her.

A good post player has to be versatile. She has to be more than a scorer, more than a rebounder. A good post player has to be able to pass the ball and block shots. She has to be able to set screens and deny passes. She has to be able to handle the ball and run the floor. A good post player has to be smart and understand the game.

I had certain God-given abilities as a player, but I was by no means a natural player. I had to constantly work hard to be a good post player.

A player cannot just show up in the gym. A coach cannot just roll out the ball. Post players need specific work to develop specific skills. In this book, I share drills I used throughout my career, from high school to the pros. I have also included drills that I use as a coach. Good basketball players and good coaches never stop learning. I still enjoy watching and listening to other coaches and players. I see new drills being used every season at every level of the game. I sincerely thank all of my former coaches for putting me through those drills and teaching me the skills I needed to play the game.

I learned a lot by playing basketball. Sports are good for everyone. Look past the medals and championships to the intangibles. There are life lessons. I learned about team concepts. I learned about playing the game with other people for a common goal. I learned about camaraderie. I learned time management. I learned how to work through difficulties, whether they be physical or mental. And I learned about dedication, discipline and hard work.

Now I hope to pass on some of what I learned.

*Anne Donovan*
*National Basketball Hall of Fame*

*chapter one*

# Post Player Conditioning

# Physical Conditioning

## *Long Distance Running*

Every athlete has to have a good foundation of conditioning. Long distance running in the off-season is a good way to build that foundation. Ask your coach for advice on how far and how long you should run, depending on your age and current physical condition. Jogging 20 to 30 minutes, three to five times a week should help you with your endurance.

In the middle of the off-season, do not worry too much about your time or distance. Just run. You should keep a pace that still allows you to carry on a conversation without too much difficulty. As you get closer to the start of your season, you should increase your pace and distance.

Make certain you wear good shoes and try to run on a soft surface such as a running track, sand, grass or a gym floor.

## *Interval Training*

Combine your long distance running with sprints to provide better overall conditioning. Jog 100 yards or so, then sprint 50 yards. Jog another 100 yards so you can catch your breath, then sprint another 50 yards. In the beginning, do that without a break for 10 minutes. Slowly build up to 20 minutes as you gain your endurance. Mix up your distances. Try sprinting 25 yards, then jogging 75. Or sprint 100 yards, then jog 200.

Add motions you use in basketball. Backpedal as fast as you can for 50 yards, followed by a jog. Sprint 20 yards with one hand over your head, looking back over your shoulder as you might on a fast break (but be careful of where you are going); jog for 50 yards.

Throw in some defensive slides, make the steal after 20 yards, then sprint 25 yards on the fast break. Be creative while working at maximum effort.

### *Running with a Ball*

Combine your long distance running with ball handling drills. Dribble a basketball as you run. If you run outside, use an old ball. If you learn to dribble around potholes, curbs and cracks in the sidewalk, dribbling on a smooth gym floor will be easy. Use both hands. Dribble with your left hand for a city block or one lap, then switch to your right hand for a block or lap. Keeping your eyes up to see where you are will help you handle a tough defensive player.

If you run on a track with a partner, one player can run in lane 1 and the other in lane 8. Pass the ball to each other all the way around the track. Try not to break stride. Count the number of passes it takes to complete a lap. Try to reduce that number the next lap. Switch places with each other after every lap. (The distance covered in lane 8 for one lap is much farther than the distance in lane 1.)

## *Suicides*

There is no escaping suicides, the running drill coaches use at every level of the game.

Start at one baseline and run to the nearest free-throw line. Touch the line, then run back to the baseline. Touch the baseline, then run and touch the center line. Return to the baseline and touch it. Run and touch the other free-throw line, then return and touch the baseline. Now run and touch the other baseline and sprint back to the original baseline.

Basketball is a series of starts and stops and suicides do a very good job of simulating the game. How many suicides do you need to do? It depends on your level of conditioning and what kind of workout you have had prior to running your suicides.

Determine the time it normally takes you to run one suicide during and after an average practice. If it is 30 seconds, then try to run every suicide in 30 seconds (with a minute or two rest in-between). If it is more than 30 seconds, that's OK. You just need someplace to start. Once you have a starting point, you can begin to set goals to better your time.

Vary your suicides. Try running them in reverse order; run the full court segment first, then end with the short sprint to the nearest free-throw line. Try running them from sideline to sideline, using the two sides of the free-throw lane as stopping points. Try running forward to the line, then backpedal back to the baseline on each segment. Or run them while dribbling a ball.

### *Stretching*

I think the most overlooked area of conditioning for basketball players is stretching. Most players get on the court, shoot around for a few minutes to loosen up, jog up and down the floor for a couple of minutes and pronounce themselves ready for practice.

All players should spend 10 to 15 minutes prior to every workout stretching their muscles. That includes in-season and off-season workouts both on and off the court; it includes regulation games and pickup contests.

Stretching helps to increase your flexibility, and I found that my joints may have been more stable because of the time I committed to stretching.

Work with your trainer or coach on specific stretches, but make certain you cover every major muscle group. Make this a part of your regular warm-up routine.

At the end of practice, following some sprint work or free throws, most players head straight to the locker room and the showers. Don't. You should spend another 10 to 15 minutes stretching again.

Stretching is an important part of staying healthy. Do not ever skip your stretching exercises.

## *Weight Training*

Strength is a much bigger factor in today's game. When I played, only the elite players were working hard in the weight room. Today, you must have a regular strength training program to be a successful player.

Work with your trainer or coach to come up with an appropriate program for you. Your workout should vary depending on whether you are in-season or off-season. Work muscles throughout your body, but spend extra time on your legs.

Studies show that female basketball players are more susceptible to knee injuries. By concentrating on equally developing both hamstring and quadriceps strength, many believe that this can reduce the risk of knee injury.

I recommend that young players use weight machines, rather than free weights. The machines are easier to use, so there are fewer injuries. However, after you gain experience and confidence in the weight room, you may consider switching to free weights. Studies have shown that free weights work a wider range of muscles than machines do. And free weights help you work on your balance, too.

Do not listen to anyone who suggests shortcuts to increased strength. There is a whole list of supplements, such as steroids, that are illegal. They are illegal because tests have shown them to be unhealthy. Do not be tempted. Shortcuts to strength could be parlayed into long term serious health problems.

Put in the time and effort required and build your muscles and strength naturally.

### *Hand/Eye Coordination*

There are a number of exercises you can use to improve hand/eye coordination. The simplest is the old-fashioned paddle ball. Bounce the ball on the string off the paddle as many times in a row as you can.

Learn to juggle three balls. Use one hand to juggle two balls. Play catch with a Frisbee. Play a full court basketball game using a tennis ball. Play Whiffle Ball or handball.

Remember to practice with both hands. It is important to develop coordination with each hand. To make your weaker hand stronger, do your daily tasks with it: eat with your weak hand, brush your hair and teeth with it.

A good drill that helps hand/eye coordination is ball taps with your fingertips. Dribble off a wall, alternating hands. Work on using your fingertips for control and quick touches on the ball. When you get good at that (and tall enough) use the backboard for your ball taps. Now you are incorporating your jumping and timing skills with your hand/eye coordination. That's a good conditioning drill, too.

## Mental Conditioning

### *Cross Training*

To avoid mental fatigue, as well as increase your overall conditioning, utilize cross training. When you tire of jogging the same route or shooting at the same outdoor hoop, try another activity.

Rollerblade or ride your bike. Swim or play tennis. Kick box or jump rope. Use the gym's rowing machine or treadmill. Take an aerobics or ballet class. Just being active is what is most important.

One of the best off-season sports for basketball players is volleyball. Just like basketball, volleyball is a series of starts and stops. There is plenty of jumping and ball handling. Coordination is developed, and there is teamwork.

Do not use cross training as an excuse to avoid work on your basketball skills. Use cross training to avoid the weariness that can come from the same workout routine day after day.

## *Nutrition*

Good nutrition is not a basketball drill, but it is as important to the physical condition of every player as any exercise routine. It has become a cliché, but it is true: You are what you eat.

Fuel your body with good foods and you will see and feel the difference. I like to think about good and bad "gas" for my body. Making sure my body runs efficiently requires the right fuel.

Good nutrition is pretty basic. We all learned it in health class. If you have questions, talk with your trainer, coach or family doctor.

If you need help losing or gaining weight, make sure you consult a specialist and follow their directions.

Besides filling your body with the proper foods, make sure you supply your body with enough fluids. Do not wait until your body is thirsty to take a drink. Keep your body hydrated at all times. Make certain you drink plenty of water before, during and after every workout and game. Skipping a water break does not make you tough. It makes you foolish.

## *Communication*

In order to become the best possible player you can be, you must study the game of basketball. Physical skills will only take you so far.

Learn to communicate with your coaches and teammates. Ask questions on and off the court. Spend time away from the court with your coach to discuss your strengths and weaknesses. Follow the coach's directions and ask for feedback. If you do not understand what a coach is trying to tell you, ask her to say it again.

Do not misconstrue coaching with criticism. Coaches may be critical in evaluating your performance, but they are doing it to make you a better player. Coaches are there to teach you and motivate you. The best coaches accentuate the positives, but there is no easy way to point out negatives. Take negative comments in stride and use them to become a better player.

Talk to older teammates who likely have experienced what you will be going through in the development of your game.

Talk on the court and talk on the bench (except when your coach is talking). If you can help a teammate with a comment, then do it. If you need to ask a question, do not be reluctant.

## *Read Basketball Books*

Read books about basketball. Read books on developing specific skills. Read books about offensive and defensive strategies. Read biographies of the greatest players and coaches.

You may not be able to figure out the proper angle of your elbow in shooting a free throw by reading a book, but you should be able to learn philosophies of the game. You may never have a chance to sit and chat with Pat Summitt or Rebecca Lobo, but you can read their books. You will be able to find out their experiences and thoughts. Glean information from successful role models.

Also read books on basketball strategy. You may not need to actually diagram a play. However, the more you understand what makes certain offensive sets work better against certain defenses, the easier it will be for you to pick up new sets that your coach teaches you. It will be easier for you to recognize that same set your opponent is running, and how to counter that.

## *Watch Video Tapes*

Almost every team video tapes its games. Watching the tape can provide a wealth of information. A coach can show you exactly what you did that was correct or incorrect. If your team's formal video session does not allow time for you to review the entire tape, ask the coach if you can watch the tape at home or spend extra time with you to review your performance.

Having someone video tape your practices or informal workouts can also be helpful.

The tape never lies. It shows exactly what you did. Wear out the pause and rewind buttons on your remote control to review specific aspects of your performance. Compare recent tapes with tapes from previous years to track your progress in different areas.

Also utilize scouting tapes. Prior to playing a game, review tape of your opponent. Watch the strengths and weaknesses of the player you will be matched against. Visualize yourself playing against that opponent. How will you stop her best move? What will you do to score against her? Watch other players on the tape, too. Does the team like to double-team when the ball goes into the low post? Where does that double-team come from?

### *Watch Instructional Videos*

Check with your coach, library or sporting goods stores for basketball instructional video tapes. Then get the tapes and watch them.

Videos have been produced by coaches and players on virtually every subject imaginable. You should be able to gain some knowledge of the game from every tape. Let Lisa Leslie describe the drop step. Let Red Auerbach teach you the basics of free- throw shooting. And let Cheryl Miller show you proper rebounding position.

Review the tapes on a regular basis.

## *Watch Other Games*

Whether in person, on TV or on tape, watch as many basketball games as you can. However, rather than watching solely for personal enjoyment, watch with a purpose.

Ask your coach what you should look for in a particular game. If it is an NBA game involving Shaquille O'Neal, you might want to observe how he uses his body to get position in the low post. (Do not watch him shoot free throws, though.) If you are watching a local college team play, you might be advised to watch how the post players set screens. Do not get caught up watching the ball all the time. Watch the players that play your position. What do they do away from the ball? What move do they make when they are forced to go left? Where do they go on the floor when they are the trailer on a fast break? How might you play the game differently?

Take notes on what you see. Diagram a move that created an easy shot for the post player. Discuss what you saw with your coach. Try to recreate that move the next day in practice. Review your notes on a regular basis.

## *Play Against Better Competition*

If you are the best player on the team, you still can — and must — improve your skills. Do not become overconfident or complacent just because you are the best player on the court at a given time. Inferior competition may exaggerate your strengths and allow your weaknesses to lay dormant.

The best way to continue improvement is to play against better competition. If you are a freshman in high school, try to play with upper classmen. If you are a senior, then try to play in the summer against college players. If you are a college player, find out where local professionals work out.

Also, do not be afraid to play against boys. Find a pick-up game of boys that slightly exceed your ability and join in. Do not choose a game where you know you will be overmatched. If you are a senior in high school, you may or may not be able to keep up with the boys on the varsity squad, but challenge yourself to compete with boys on the freshman or sophomore teams.

## *Diagram Plays*

Too often basketball players figure the only ones who need to know what everyone on the floor is doing are the coaches and point guards. Wrong.

Every player should know what every other player is doing during every offensive and defensive set. Knowing what everyone else is doing will allow you to make proper adjustments if the play breaks down.

It also will make you a more valuable player. You can step in for a player who is injured or in foul trouble. It may allow you to play more minutes and develop more skills. Playing someone else's position for a brief time will also make you a better post player. For example, if you spend some time on the wing trying to pass into the low post, you can see how important it is to be a big a target when posting up. You can see how important it is to keep the defender behind you. When you go back to the post, you will know exactly what the wing is seeing and thinking.

Spend time diagramming your team's plays. Check with your coach to make certain you are doing it correctly. Save the diagrams. You never know when you may be coaching someday.

You can take "quizzes" with your teammates. You give her a few plays to diagram and vice versa. The winner has bragging rights ... until the next time.

### *Keep a Journal*

Take a couple of minutes at the end of each day to write down what you accomplished that day.

If you are in-season, write down what you learned at practice and what you worked on. If you had a game, write down what you did that was good and what you need to work on. If you are in the off-season, write down the conditioning drills and specific basketball skills you worked on. If you shot 100 free throws, keep track of how many you made. If you watched a game or read a basketball book, chronicle aspects you deem important. If you are trying to gain or lose weight, monitor the food you ate. If you hear a good motivational line, record it. How did you feel physically and mentally?

Review your journal on a regular basis. Make sure you follow up on items. Relive your good games and recall tips you read.

*chapter two*

# Post Offense

# Positioning

## *Work on Proper Footwork*

Good footwork is essential for good post players. Footwork must become natural, not mechanical. Only through repetitive drills will your footwork be natural.

The first piece of footwork to work on is establishing a pivot foot. Most young players prefer to always use the same foot as their pivot foot. That usually is the foot opposite of their dominant hand. Why? If you are right-handed and you use your left foot as your pivot foot, it is easier to square up into your shot or dribble with your right hand, or have momentum when executing a crossover move.

You must learn to move either direction from either pivot foot so your defender cannot overplay you. You must do this facing the basket or with your back to the basket.

The only way to perfect these moves is to practice. Have someone throw you a pass from different angles or toss the ball out a couple of steps and go retrieve it yourself. If you catch the ball away from the basket, pivot on your inside foot to get into the triple threat position. If you pivot with your left foot, the triple threat position has your right foot slightly ahead of your left with your feet shoulder width apart. You are slightly crouched with the ball on the right side of your chest. Make certain you are protecting the ball from your defender. From this position, you are a triple threat: you are in position to shoot, pass or dribble. You must be able to do any of the three regardless of which foot is your pivot foot. So if you pivot with your left foot, your left foot will be slightly in front of your right foot, etc.

By yourself, practice each option (shooting, passing, dribbling) off each pivot foot. Practice going to your left and to your right. Practice going straight up for a shot. Practice throwing a variety of passes from that position. Practice a fake before you complete your pass, dribble or shot.

When you become proficient, try it with a defender. Have the defender play loosely in the beginning and tighten up as you become more comfortable with the moves. This positioning and footwork is something players of all ages should work on throughout their careers. Developing both right and left feet is as important as developing your right and left hands.

## *Establishing Position in the Low Post*

To be an offensive threat, post players must be able to score from the low post. That's the area about six feet from the rim in every direction. Good post players must be able to score facing the basket or with a dribble-drive to the basket going left or right. Exceptional post players also can score with a jump shot or hook shot from a variety of angles. All post players must also be able to pass to an open cutter or a spot-up shooter from the post area.

The first step is establishing position. You want to establish a position as close to the basket as you can (without being called for a three-second lane violation). And you want to create a target or passing angle for your teammate to get you the ball. To establish position, you must know where your defender is. If your defender is between you and the basket, your best chance of receiving a pass is to have your back to the basket and your defender. However, you must always know where your defender is. Is she cheating to your left or right? Is she backing off you or trying to push you farther out on the floor? To know where your defender is, you either have to turn around and look or you have to be able to feel her. Since it is impossible to catch a pass in the low post with your head turned away, the easiest way to know the location of your defender is to continually make contact with her. Use your rear end or a hip to back into your defender. Let your rear end be the eyes in your back. Your object is to make and maintain contact, but not to knock her over. Do not foul her. And know where you are in relation to the free-throw lane and basket at all times. With practice, you also can use the back of your arm to check your defender's location and keep her behind you. Do not grab or hold with your hand. You want to establish a good, solid base. Plant your feet a little wider than shoulder width, maintaining your balance and a strong stance at all times. Spread out your shoulders and think BIG! Make yourself big, but don't leave your feet in wet cement. You have to remain on the balls of your feet, ready to move any direction.

Now you need to create a target. You always should keep as much of your body as you can between the target and your defender. If your defender is directly behind you, place one or both of your hands in front of your face. Call for the ball. That is where your teammate should throw the ball. If your defender is shading your right side, put out your left hand to create a target that keeps your body between the target and the defender. If the defender plays in front of you, then create the target in a straight line to the basket. The passer can throw the ball over the defender's head in a direct line to the basket. This is called a lob pass.

To practice establishing position, have a defender play you a variety of ways. Sometimes she can play directly behind you, sometimes on your right side or left side, sometimes directly in front of you. Work at making contact with the defender and creating a target away from the defender. Have a teammate throw you the ball from a variety of angles. Do not shoot the ball yet. Use this drill just to establish position, feel your defender and create a target.

Get used to the contact and maintain your concentration. The bigger you make yourself, the easier it will be for the passer to get you the ball in position to score.

## *Establishing Position at the High Post*

The high post is usually described as the area along the free-throw line or at the sides of the lane near the free-throw line. Establishing position at the high post is essentially the same as the low post.

You must know where your defender is. The best way to know is to initiate and maintain contact with your defender. Create a target for the passer away from the defender.

To practice, get a defender to play you a number of different ways: directly behind you, on your right, on your left, directly in front of you. Initiate and maintain the contact, think BIG, then create a target. Move to another area in the high post and repeat.

Once you are comfortable with those positions, move from one spot to another both at the high post and low post. Work hard at knowing where the defender is at all times and work at creating a target.

### *Cutting*

As a post player you will not always be positioned next to the basket. You may occasionally find yourself farther out on the floor. You need to learn how to effectively cut to and from the basket to get yourself open.

When you make a cut, think "straight line." Think "sharp angle" not "curve." A good drill to practice cuts is the V-cut. From the wing, run in a straight line to the basket, change direction and speed as quickly as you can and return to the wing. Your path should form the letter "V." Your path should not resemble the shape of a banana. Now from the wing, break to the baseline, change direction and move to the high post. Again, the path should be a "V."

When cutting, you want to beat your defender to a spot. I have found that running hard at my defender's feet and then cutting sharply away will give me the time, space and momentum to receive a pass. You can practice cutting by yourself from one point on the floor to another. First, set your defender up by taking her away from where you want to go. Then attempt to "get to her feet." From there, make a hard, quick pivot out to the spot where you want the ball. Remember to catch and square up into that triple threat position off your pivot.

Add someone to throw you the ball to work on making a target, too.

## *Setting Screens*

All post players must know how to set effective screens. You will be called on to set screens to free up the shooters on your team.

Know the basics. In setting a screen, first protect yourself. Keep your elbows in, bringing your forearms into your chest. Set your feet a little wider than shoulder width, bend your knees and hold your position. The rule is that you have to give the defender one step, so do not get directly on top of the person you are screening. Know the timing of the play. Do not set the screen too early. Go to a position a step away from the defender. Let your teammate run her defense into you. Do not lunge at the defender. Do not stick out an arm or hip to brush the defender. Your teammate should try to rub shoulders with you so that there is no way the defender can slide between you and your teammate. The defender should be forced to trail your teammate around the screen or duck under the screen. After you set the screen, you should roll to the basket, keeping your eyes on the ball handler. More times than not, the screener is the person who actually winds up open. Look to receive a pass every time you set a screen and roll.

To practice setting screens, start with screening a stationary object, such as a chair. Set the screen a step away from the chair, let your teammate cut off you by brushing shoulders, then roll to the basket. Eventually, add a real defender to screen.

Setting a good screen takes practice and good technique. Do not get lazy. A good screen is as valuable as a good pass, and it is the key to getting players open.

## *Using a Screen*

Post players need to know how to use a screen to help them get open.

You must set up your defender when using a screen. If you are cutting without the ball, take a quick jab step away from the screen before running directly to the screen. Brush shoulders with the screener so that the defender cannot get between you and the screener. If the screener's defender steps out to block your path, avoid contact with the defender and cut away from her to an open space. If the defenders do not switch, continue to an open area of the court or directly to the basket. It is up to you to run your defender into the screen. The screener is not allowed to move once she has established position, so you must brush shoulders with the screener to utilize the tactic.

Practice first without a defender. Take a few steps away from the screen, cut to the screen, rub shoulders and continue on. Add a defender on you. Have the defender trail you over the top and determine your best course of action. Then have your defender cut under the screen. Where is the best place for you to go? Add a defender on the screener. Have that defender switch out on you. Where is the open spot on the floor then?

# Ball Handling

## *Dribbling*

There are hundreds of drills to help you become a better dribbler. The bottom line is: you must constantly practice dribbling with each hand against a defender to become a better dribbler.

To begin, just practice dribbling up and down the court without a defender. Use your left hand to go the length of the court, then use your right hand to come back. Keep your body low to the ground so the ball does not have to travel a great distance between the floor and your hand. Use your fingertips, not the palm of your hand. Do not look at the ball. Keep your head up, so you can watch the other players on the court. Your touch on the ball should be light, but you should maintain total control of the ball at all times. Your dribble should be strong.

When you become proficient at dribbling in a straight line, place chairs or cones on the court and practice weaving in and out of those obstacles. Then practice the crossover dribble, switching from the left hand to the right hand and the right to the left.

Add a defender. Begin by turning your body slightly and using it to help you ward off the defender. Learn to go left and right with your body between the ball and defender, rather than backing your way up the court. Then try dribbling while facing the defender. Use your crossover dribble and drive past the defender.

Once you can accomplish the basic dribble, learn to use the dribble to get to the basket. Use a power drive to the basket from the wing or high post. Practice without a defender until you can go to the basket at full speed, but under control. Learn to go up for a lay-up or come to a stop for a shot.

## *Passing the Ball*

There are four basic passes that every basketball player, regardless of position, should master. If you are practicing alone, throw passes at a target on the wall. If you have a partner, simply throw passes back and forth, changing the distance with each pass.

The most common pass is a two-handed chest pass. Start with your hands holding the ball firmly at your chest. Your fingertips should do the work, not your palms. Spread out your fingers comfortably on the ball with your thumbs downward. Push the ball forward with both hands while taking a step toward the target. As you extend your arms, snap the ball so your palms swing out, facing away from each other. The power comes equally from your arms and leg stepping forward. Aim for your teammate's chest. Learn to throw this pass various distances and various speeds.

The two-handed overhead pass begins with you raising the ball over your head. Place a hand on both sides of the ball with your thumbs positioned on the back of the ball. Keep the ball above your head. Do not move it behind your head for leverage. Step toward your target and push the ball. Your hands should follow through extended in front of your chest with your palms facing downward and slightly out. Work on throwing this pass various distances and various speeds.

In the one-handed baseball pass, the ball is brought up to your shoulder area with two hands. As you move to pass, rotate to your outside slightly, raise the ball to your passing shoulder, and move the ball to your outside hand. As the ball comes up to the side of your head, step toward the target and throw your arm straight out. Follow through after you complete the pass, with your palm facing downward, but your extended arm at least shoulder height. Learn to throw this pass with accuracy as far down the court as you can.

The bounce pass can be thrown a number of different ways. The most common bounce passes are thrown with the two-handed chest pass motion or a sidearm one-handed baseball throw. Learn to throw this pass from a variety of angles with each hand. Experiment with different angles of release and see how it affects the bounce of the ball.

There are other types of passes that need perfecting, but all utilize the skills necessary for these four basic passes. Practice, practice and practice. Practice from a standing position. Practice hitting a moving target. Practice passing off the dribble. Practice passing to the wing. Practice passing into the post. Practice making the outlet pass on the fast break. Practice a fake before making your pass. My high school coach used to say, "Fake the pass to make the pass." That is a good idea, especially against tough defenders.

When starting out, practice your passing using a simple weave. Have three players run down the court, passing and cutting behind the player you pass to. End the drill by shooting a layup. Concentrate on making crisp passes, no "floaters."

Then use one defender and a teammate to play keep-away, utilizing a full range of passes from various distances. Put the defender on you and practice making passes to your open teammate. Put the defender on your teammate in various positions. Practice passing to your teammate from various distances and various angles. Add a second defender. Have the defenders apply soft pressure at first, then pick up the pressure as you become more experienced. You must practice protecting the ball, using good pivots and stepping around the defender to complete the pass.

## *Catching the Ball*

As simple as it sounds, catching the basketball is an acquired skill that all players need to continue to practice. Only through repetitive work will a player become proficient at catching the ball.

If you are alone, throw a ball against a wall or portable backstop. Learn to catch the ball with your hands. Absorb the force of the pass with your wrists and arms. Do not let the ball ricochet off your fingertips. Your hands must be soft, ready to receive the ball. If your hands are rigid, the ball is likely to bounce off or be fumbled.

Most players are able to catch well-thrown passes. The mark of a good catcher is a player who can handle errant passes. The only way to consistently catch bad passes is to practice catching them. While in position in the low post, have someone throw you the ball from the wing. Throw the pass low and away, then high and wide. Learn to stop the ball with one hand, then control it by bringing the other hand over to cover it.

Learn to go get the ball. Do not wait for the ball to come to you. You should beat your defender to the ball. Never give the defender the opportunity to knock the ball away before you get to it. Hold off your defender with good positioning until you are able to receive the pass. Once you catch the ball, hang on with both hands and move it immediately to your chest.

It is important to keep your eyes on the ball. Look the ball into your hands. Practice with someone trying to distract you. Have them stand in front of you, blocking part of your vision. Have them wave their arms in front of your face in an attempt to make you lose your concentration. To increase your reaction time, turn away from a passer, turn on her call, and catch the pass that has already been released. Try catching passes with one hand held behind your back.

Remember, after catching the ball, you will want to read the defense quickly. Your defender will help you determine whether you move into the triple threat position or perhaps make a quick move to the basket.

## Shooting

### *Layups*

The most basic shot in basketball is the layup. Yet, players at all levels miss the shot in games because of bad form, sloppiness or lost concentration.

There are two kinds of lay-ups. One is the running layup and the other is the power layup.

Here are the rules for the running layup:

1) Unless you are tall enough to drop the ball straight through the basket, you will look to bank the ball off the backboard. That said, your best move is driving to one side of the basket or the other, not directly in front of the rim.
2) Learn to use both hands equally well.
3) When shooting with your right hand, always lift your right leg to help propel your body up to the basket.
4) When shooting with your left hand, always lift your left leg to help propel your body up to the basket.

To practice your layups, do a three-person weave. You can do it full court or half court. If you are alone, dribble from the free-throw line to the basket and shoot a layup. Recover the shot from the net before it hits the ground, dribble back to the free throw, reverse and drive to the basket using the opposite hand. Repeat. Add your ball handling moves to make your layup practice more game like. Visualize beating your defender off a crossover move and go in for the winning layup.

Post players are wise to perfect the reverse layup as well. This move is especially effective if you find yourself pushed too far underneath the basket and you still have a dribble to use. The reverse layup means you cross under the basket, near the baseline. You use your outside hand to dribble away from the defender and come up on the opposite side of the rim. Using the backboard and practicing the angles will be important in order to master this shot.

The power layup is taken from a two-footed stance. It is an effective shot when you find yourself too far under the basket. With the power layup, you can jump from a steady base toward the basket. A power layup is also a great shot to have when playing against players who are stronger than you are. This shot allows you to have more balance, strength (because you will power up off two feet) and control.

### *Tip-ins*

Post players can pick up a lot of baskets if they become proficient with tip-ins. Depending on your size and jumping ability, tip-ins can be a very good weapon for you. Do not take tip-ins for granted. Practice the tip-in on a regular basis.

You can practice the shot alone. Simply toss the ball off the backboard. Jump up and gain control of the ball with one or two hands (depending on your strength and coordination). Before you return to the ground, tip or shoot the ball back into the basket. Make sure you have control of the ball. If you do not have complete control of the ball, do not attempt to tip it in. Instead, come back down to the ground with the ball, gather yourself and go right back up for an easy follow-up.

To gain your timing and coordination, practice using your fingertips to tap the ball off the backboard. Tap the ball 10 times and on the 11th, tip the ball in. Then switch hands. As you become better, increase your goals. How many can you do? Try alternating hands. Tap with your right, then with your left until you execute the tip-in.

## *Jump Shots*

Most points in games today are scored via a jump shot. Amazingly, the jump shot did not become a regular part of the game until 50 years after the game's creation. Prior to that, players routinely took set shots or sweeping hook shots.

The mechanics of a jump shot are simple. Put the ball to your forehead, just in front of your eye on your shooting side, jump straight up, push the ball toward the basket with your shooting hand and follow through with your arm extended upward and your hand waving "goodbye."

In truth, very seldom does a player have a wide open jump shot when the simple mechanics can be used. Often, the shot is attempted while you are on the move. To be a good shooter in games, you must practice under gamelike conditions.

Start from a specific spot on the court where your offense may create a shot opportunity for you. Make a V-cut and return to that spot, catch a pass, square up and go straight into your shot. Repeat the drill for a series of shots. Move to another spot on the floor. Repeat the drill. Make fatigue a factor. In most games, fatigue plays a part, especially late in the game. Continue the drill, changing spots on the floor. Keep track of your makes and misses and record the results. Attempt to improve your performance over time.

To add variety, start at the wing. Shoot a jump shot. As a rebounder retrieves the ball, run and touch the sideline and return to your spot. Catch a pass from the rebounder and shoot again. Go touch the sideline and return to the spot. Mix up the spots and mix up the lines. Sometimes run to the sideline and sometimes run to the baseline or centerline.

Practice taking turnaround and fade-away jump shots in the low post. Begin without a defender, then add one. Always do it at full speed.

## *Bank Shots*

The bank shot is the most underutilized shot in the game today. Studies have shown that shooting percentages increase when the backboard is used. However, it takes a lot of practice to be able to use the backboard properly for bank shots.

You should practice bank shots from a variety of spots on the court to understand the angles involved. Use the white box painted on the board to help you find a target. You want to shoot high in that square for the bank shot. Remember, you do not want to bang the ball off the backboard. You want to "kiss" the ball off the glass.

During scrimmages, try to use the backboard for any shot you take that is not along the baseline or from a line extending between the two baskets. The more you shoot the bank shot, the more comfortable you will feel using it and the more successful you will become using it.

### *Hook Shot*

Most post players should develop some kind of hook shot. Not everyone is able to shoot a wide, sweeping sky hook à la Kareem Abdul-Jabbar. But post players should be able to shoot a one-handed hook, or baby hook originating from shoulder level.

In a one-on-one match-up, a well-executed hook shot is the hardest shot to block. Perfect a short hook around the basket using each hand. If you are an undersized post player, this shot is a must for you.

Begin close to the basket without a defender. Add range and gradually shoot against a defender. Use it in scrimmages, and when you are comfortable with it, use it in a game.

## *Avoiding Blocked Shots*

Post players usually are matched up against the opposing team's tallest players. If you are shorter than your defender, you may find it difficult to get off your shots. If you are the tallest player on your team, you may not be used to someone swatting away your shots.

A common drill to help you shoot over a taller opponent is to provide your practice defender with an extended reach. She can use a tennis racquet or a broom or anything else that will simulate a long arm reaching over you. Practice your turnaround jump shots over it. Practice your hook shots. Get used to the long arm in practice and it won't seem quite as imposing during a game.

For post players who have a size disadvantage, do not become discouraged or intimidated. If you are smaller, you are probably quicker. This is your advantage. To avoid having your shots blocked, make quick moves around the taller defender.

## *Get Three-Point Plays*

There is a lot of contact around the basket. Get used to it. The stronger you become and the more you practice around contact, the less distracting it becomes.

Be a threat to convert three-point plays by playing through the contact. Have a defender grab or slap your arm or nudge your body while you work on your shots around the basket. If you fight through the contact and concentrate on finishing the shot, you will surprise even yourself with how many three-point opportunities you get. Do not be satisfied with just drawing a shooting foul. Concentrate on making the field goal.

## *Free Throws*

There are two ways to practice free-throw shooting. Both methods are required to maximize your ability to hit a high percentage of your shots.

You first must develop a routine. Watch the best free-throw shooters in the WNBA and NBA. They all have a consistent and repetitive routine. Most have flawless form. Create that routine and form by shooting thousands of free throws.

Figure out what relaxes you and puts you in the right frame of mind at the line. Position yourself square to the basket. If you are right handed, your right foot will be slightly in front of the left. Take the ball from the official and visualize your shot with a successful result. Take a deep breath. If you want to bounce the ball a time or two, do so, but bounce the ball the same number of times on each attempt. Put the ball to your forehead in a straight line between your eyes and the middle of the rim. I like to have the knees bent so that there is just one motion upward. Extend your arm and shoot the ball toward the rim. Follow through with a wave to the basket. With the proper arc, the ball should travel straight to the basket. With a bit of backspin, the ball will either swish through the net or dance softly on the rim and roll in. Repeat the routine. If you want to wipe your hands on your socks or brush your hand on the side of your face or pull an earlobe as a signal to your loved ones in the stands, go ahead. Just do it every time.

Video tape your shot and observe your motion on shots you made and those you missed. Try to repeat the motion of your made shots. Shoot at least 100 free throws a day and record your results. Try to improve daily. My goal is always to "swish it." I know it is a perfect shot if the ball touches only the net on the way through the basket.

That's how you acquire proper form. Making free throws in a game is a different story. In a game you are fatigued and may be under pressure. To become a better free-throw shooter in games, you have to recreate that situation as much as you can during practice. How? Sprint the length of the court before attempting your free throws so you feel a bit winded. Remember that you have 10 seconds to shoot. Use as much or little of that time as you need. Never try more than two free throws at a time without running another sprint or at least stepping away from the line. That's how you practice with fatigue. Now, how do you create pressure?

Keep track of your shooting percentage. Offer a prize to the player who makes the highest percentage in practice. Run wind sprints, then select one player to shoot a pair of free throws. If the player makes both free throws, everyone stops running and practice is over. If the player misses either free throw, the players run again. Then another player is selected to shoot two free throws.

Run a couple of sprints. Divide the team equally at two baskets. Have each player shoot two free throws. The team that makes the most shots gets to sit out the next sprint while the losing team has to run again. Or make each team run sprints equal to the number of shots they missed.

Play a game of "21." Score one point for each made free throw and subtract two for each free throw missed. Divide into two teams and let each player take two free throws at a time. The first team to 21 wins.

Free throws. Think form and pressure. Find a way to do both, and you are on the way to shooting a high percentage.

*chapter three*

# Post Defense

## Positioning

### *Low Post Defense*

Go back to the section in this book that describes getting offensive positioning in the low post. It says that the key is to initiate and maintain contact with the defender. So, it seems within reason that the best way to defend a player in the low post is to avoid that contact. Having minimal contact will allow you to be quicker to deny passes into the post or deflect the pass.

Do not let the offensive player know exactly where you are. You may be directly behind the player. You may be shading her left side or right side. That does not mean you are so far away from the offensive player that she has time to catch a pass, turn and shoot before you can recover. It means that you can reach out and touch her because you should be no farther away than arm's distance.

You have a strong arm bar, your forearm, that makes contact with the offensive player and allows you to keep the distance you want from her. You do not want your feet too close to the offensive player. You will get pinned too easily if that happens. As she moves toward you, a good defensive player will use the arm bar to control the offensive player and maintain a smart distance.

The best drill for practicing defensive positioning is called Bull in the Ring. You need two to four passers scattered around the perimeter and someone to play offense against you. The perimeter players pass the ball around and the offensive player cuts to the ball in the low post. A good defender moves as the ball moves and always keeps an arm or body between the ball and her man. You want to prevent the offensive player an easy direct cut to the ball. Force the offensive player to take another path to the ball. Occasionally, a perimeter player can throw the ball into the post, but the key to the drill is maintaining solid defensive positioning while the ball is in different positions and your man is cutting to the ball.

One exception to avoiding contact is if your coach's strategy is to play in front of the offensive player. If so, you will need to maintain contact with the offensive player via your butt, hip, or arm, so you will know when she moves to another area of the court. When you front a post player, it is important to not allow too much space between you and your offensive player.

### *High Post Defense*

The rules in defending the high post area are essentially the same as the low post, in that you want to discourage the pass to the player you are guarding. You want to deny her the ball and not allow easy cuts to the ball. The free-throw line area is a well-used area by post players. Many teams use their high post to reverse the ball in their offense. It is important to force the offense to work to make that pass.

One difference is that if the offensive player is not a good shooter, you might play off her a bit. Then you will be in a better position to play help defense and get an edge at getting to a backboard on a missed shot.

You can run the Bull in the Ring drill to practice defending the high post, too.

# Individual

## *Man-to-Man Defenses*

The basic defense at all levels of play is the man-to-man. If you have a good foundation in playing man-to-man, you will easily adapt to a zone or other trick defenses.

The key to being a good defender is determination. You must be determined at all times to stop your opponent. If your assignment is to deny your opponent the ball, then you must be determined to accomplish that. If your assignment is to force your opponent away from the basket, then you must be determined to do that.

Playing good defense is hard work. The defensive end of the court is not the place to rest if you are tired. The defensive end is not the place to celebrate a good move or key basket at the other end of the court. When you are on the defensive end of the court, you must concentrate, work hard and be determined.

The basic skills are to be active, take up a lot of space, communicate with your teammates and be observant of everything around you.

To practice proper footwork and get into good physical shape, the Slide Drill is a good exercise.

Keep your hands up and move laterally for several steps as quickly as you can without crossing one leg over the other. Do not actually slide; take short choppy steps as quickly as you can. You should maintain your balance at all times and be prepared to move any direction at any moment. Have a coach blow a whistle or motion with their hand the direction they want you to move. Stay light on your feet, keep your hands and waist high, looking for an opportunity to steal the ball. Keep your eyes moving and be ready to change directions quickly.

Do not get caught flat-footed on defense. Do not get surprised by something happening behind you. You must be able to play the game with excellent floor vision. You need to see that screen before you run into it. You need to see your teammate being beaten on a drive before her man scores.

## Blocking Shots

Very few players actually practice blocking shots, but it can be such a defensive weapon that post players can find benefit in practicing it. Remember, you cannot block every shot taken by the other team, so use good judgment as to when to attempt to block a shot.

It makes for a good TV highlight to swat a shot into the fourth row of the bleachers, but that should not be your objective. Yes, your first goal is to get a piece of the ball, and if that means the ball is deflected out of bounds, so be it. However, your second objective is to block the shot and keep the ball in play. Giving yourself or your teammates an opportunity to recover the ball might mean two points at the other end.

It also is important not to foul the offensive player while attempting to block a shot. When trying to block a shot, you should jump straight up and extend your arm straight up. Do not fling your arm at the ball or attempt to smash the ball back into the face of the shooter. The follow-through of your arm will likely make contact with the shooter and a foul can be called. Shooters generally get the benefit of doubt. If there is contact on a shot, most times the defender will be called for the foul.

Sometimes it will be obvious that you have no chance of actually blocking the shot. You still should try to distract the shooter. You should try to put a hand in front of the shooter's eyes. Running past the shooter can be distracting, but it does not leave you in a good position for a rebound should the shot be missed.

A good drill to practice blocking shots is to have two players line up on opposite sides of the lane line. As one player shoots, attempt to block the shot, trying to keep the ball in play. After your attempt, make sure you establish a good rebounding position against the shooter, then race over to the other player and attempt to block her shot. Keep alternating shooters. Practice reading shot fakes. You should never leave your feet to block a shot unless the ball is actually being shot.

## *Defending a Baseline Inbounds Pass*

As a post player, you may be the tallest player on your team. If so, then you are the biggest obstacle your team can put in front of an opposing player throwing an inbounds pass from the baseline.

If you are assigned the responsibility of guarding the person throwing in the ball from under the other team's basket, take that responsibility seriously. Do not just stand there with your hands raised. You should jump around, trying to take away the passer's field of vision. Watch the passer's eyes. It is easy to fake a pass with your hands and arms in a direction you are not looking, but very few passers will attempt a no-look pass from out-of-bounds. Get as close to the baseline as the officials will allow. The closer you are, the better you can reduce the passing lanes.

If your coach does not give you specific instructions, always be aware of defending the opposite block on out of bounds plays. If the ball is being thrown in from the left block, many out of bounds plays are designed to free up a player on the right block. If you can, cheat a little in that direction to make that pass more difficult to make. This will be a help to your teammates. When the ball is put into play, however, you must quickly defend your man again.

Remember, though, you should not get so involved in jumping around that you allow the passer to inbound the ball then run past you and establish good position. As soon as the ball is inbounded, establish your defensive presence in the post.

Practice defending the inbounds pass. Have the passer vary her fakes and targets. Be quick, be big, be active.

## *Defending Screens*

Different coaches have different philosophies concerning screens. Follow your coach's guidelines on defending screens.

Some coaches like the screener's defender to jump out and impede the progress of the person using the screen. That can result in a temporary or permanent double-team.

Other coaches like to switch defenders on a screen. Some even prefer you fight through the screen and avoid any switches or double-teams.

Coaches may have different rules for different areas of the court and different rules for different times in the game. Always adhere to your coach's strategy. The one common thread all coaches will teach is talking about the screen early. You must call "screen" loudly as soon as you see it being set. If you can call which side it is being set on, that's even better.

Whatever the strategy, you must practice it. You need three other players to effectively practice. Have two players on offense alternating screens on various parts of the court. You should use a ball during part of the drill, but work just as often on defending screens away from the ball. Work hard, whether you are defending the screener or the player using the screen. Determination and desire are the rules. And you must communicate with your teammate. Practice calling out the screen and follow your coach's instructions on how they want it defended.

## Team

### *Traps and Double-Teams*

Good defenses utilize traps and double-teams. There is more to a trap or double-team than putting two defenders on a player with the ball. Good double-teams require teamwork and practice.

The objective of a double-team is to force an offensive player into a difficult situation resulting, hopefully, in a turnover or poor shot.

Double-teams can be played two different ways:

1) When the offensive player still has her dribble, and
2) When the offensive player has picked up her dribble.

In the first situation, you must be more cautious and not allow the player to split or dribble out of the trap. In the dead ball trap, you are looking to create a box with no possible escape.

The proper technique for a trap is to have the defensive players touching toes perpendicularly, setting up a 90-degree angle. (One defender's left toes are touching the right toes of the other defender.) Keep your hands up and do not allow the offensive player to split between the two defenders. The defenders must block a path to the basket and must block as many passing lanes as possible.

The best double-teams take place next to a sideline, baseline or centerline, effectively creating a third and possible fourth defender.

A simple drill is to work with two other players. One player is on offense and picks a spot on the floor. A defender signals for the double-team and the other defender approaches to create the double-team. Concentrate on the execution with your teammate and your angles.

You must know when your team is going to double-team or trap. When you are moving to trap, you will go hard and fast, creating the double-team as quickly as possible. Remember, if you double-team an opponent, someone else on the offensive team will be open. Your team's strategy will be to make that open man a difficult target to find.

## *Help*

As a post player, you usually are the last line of defense. It is your responsibility to help your teammates by defending the basket. Your first priority is not giving up an easy basket to anyone. Take pride in defending your basket.

Do not blame one defender or another when an offensive player scores. It is the responsibility of the team to keep the offense from scoring. You must move off the offensive player you are covering if another player is going to the basket uncontested.

Most coaching philosophies use a rotation for help defense. You will be called on to help in many situations. In help defense, you may end up guarding a player away from the basket and not at your position. You will have to be versatile and aware of everything that is happening on the court. You will need to be prepared to help your teammates whenever they need you.

Work in practice on help and recovering to your man. Be ready to switch to another player to give your team the best chance of defending the basket.

## *2-on-1*

You may occasionally find yourself defending a 2-on-1 situation. There are two basic rules:

1) Stop the ball, and
2) Do not allow anyone to get behind you.

Never let the player bringing the ball down the floor drive to the basket uncontested. You must force the player to pick up her dribble and shoot from the outside, dribble away from the basket or make a pass.

Do not backpedal too far toward the basket. Do not allow the ball handler to force you deep into the lane. Meet the dribbler 10-12 feet from the basket and force her hand. Take a jab step toward her, fake guarding her and retreat into the passing lane. You want to slow her down. If she tries to throw a pass to the other offensive player, make the attempt as difficult as possible. If the pass is made, hurry to cover the player receiving the pass.

You want to delay the offensive players until help arrives from your teammates. The slightest hesitation on the part of an offensive player may allow your team to even up the numbers.

A good 2-on-1 drill that gets everyone on the team involved in defending and handling the ball requires the full court. Two players start on offense at midcourt. One player is stationed in the lane at both ends of the court as the original defenders. The remainder of the team is split into two even lines out of bounds at half court. The two offensive players try to score. After they make a shot, turn the ball over, or the defensive player grabs a rebound, the defender throws an outlet pass to the player first in line on the nearest sideline. She turns and heads the other way, along with the first player in the other line. One of the offensive players at the other end remains as the one defender. The other two players get at the backs of the lines at center court. Keep alternating ends of the court with full-court action.

## *3-on-2*

One important rule for defending a 3-on-2 situation is the same as the 2-on-1: Stop the ball.

The two defenders should try to work as a tandem. Get one defender in front of the other. The lead defender should harass the ball handler to do one of three things:

1) To pick up her dribble 15-20 feet from the basket,
2) Slow her down, or
3) Force her to make the pass.

Once that player passes to a teammate, the back defender must go and cover that offensive player. She approaches the ball wisely as she wants to allow time for her teammate, the lead defender, to get back and guard the basket. The lead defender drops down the middle of the lane as big as she can, into the passing lane.

Once again, your objective is to delay the offense until help arrives and the numbers become equal.

A simple team drill allows you to practice 3-on-2 and 2-on-1 situations simultaneously. Start with two defenders at one end of the court and three lines of "offensive" players out of bounds under the opposite basket. The three offensive players work their way into the front court and try to score against the two defenders (a 3-on-2 break). After the offense scores or the defenders successfully stop the offense, the two defenders retrieve the ball and run a fast break toward the other end of the court. The offensive player to last touch the ball (on a shot or turnover) retreats to defend the opposite goal (setting up a 2-on-1 break). Meanwhile, the other two original offensive players remain at that end of the court to defend against the next 3-on-2 break. After the 2-on-1 break is complete, three new players head down the court for a new 3-on-2. Repeat. Keep track of offensive baskets and defensive stops. Set goals depending on that day's priority.

*chapter four*

# Post Rebounding

### *Positioning*

Being a good rebounder is about size. No, it's not about the height or width of a player, but about the size of a player's heart. Being a good rebounder requires tenacity and a desire to go get the ball. Still, there are some basic rules every good rebounder follows.

You must recognize angles. You must know percentages. If a shot is taken from 15 feet out along either baseline, where will the ball bound if the shot is missed? Studies show that most shots bounce straight back toward the shooter or directly opposite the shooter. Why? If the shot is short and hits the closest side of the rim, the ball will bounce back to the shooter. If the shot is a bit long and hits the inside of the of the rim opposite the shooter, it will bound back to the shooter, too. If the shot comes down on top of any part of the rim, the momentum of the ball likely will cause the ball to bound away in a straight line from the shooter. The longer the shot, the longer the rebound likely will be.

Since we are dealing with a round ball, a round basket and a round metal rim, there always are exceptions to the rule. But grab a shot chart and the video tape of any basketball game. Chart every missed shot. Show the location of the shot and the direction the rebound headed. You will not have scientific data from just one game, but chances are good that you will see a pattern.

Memorize that pattern until it becomes instinctual. As shots go up, try to gauge whether they are going to short or long. That also will help you determine the direction of the rebound.

When a shot goes up, it is helpful to you and your teammates to call "shot." This is a trigger to think "rebound." Reboundinng is a habit — a very beneficial skill that coaches know to be valuable.

### *Blocking Out*

Besides being tenacious and knowing angles, another characteristic of good rebounders is the ability to block out.

It is important that as a shot is being taken you put your body between the basket and the closest opposing player. Establish position in front of the opposition and hold your ground. Make a good base with your feet spread and get your hands up. If you feel your opponent trying to move around you, adjust your position to keep your body between her and the basket.

Watch the flight of the ball and try to determine the direction of the carom. Then go get the ball.

The only way to develop a good technique in blocking out is to practice it every time a shot is taken in any drill, scrimmage or game. If you are 20 feet from the basket, you must still work to remain between your man and the basket. No matter where you are when the shot goes up, you must think, "Box out first."

Conversely, if your opponent has inside position on you and is attempting to block you out, you must fight through or around the block out. You can spin off the contact to regain your advantage. Do not foul your opponent. Avoid the contact from your opponent and move past her toward the rim.

## *Grab the Ball with Authority*

When you get a rebound, do not routinely pull it down with one hand or try to tip it to a teammate. Grab the ball with authority and immediately gain control of it with both hands.

Your opponent will be trying to knock the ball loose. Do not allow her to do so. As soon as you can, pivot away from your opponent. If you are on the offensive end, gather yourself and go strong to the basket. If you are on the defensive end, look for a possible outlet pass to create a fast break opportunity. If a fast break situation does not exist, find a safe pass to make to a guard before the opposition can double-team you. The best outlet passes in traffic are made to the outside of the court.

Practice grabbing rebounds with both hands. If you are under your own basket, make a strong move up to the goal. If you are on the defensive end, establish your pivot foot and look to make a pass as quickly as you can. If your outlet is having trouble getting open and you are facing pressure, you will want to take a power dribble away from the middle of the court.

## *Keep the Ball Up*

If you grab an offensive rebound, do not get lazy and bring the ball back down to your waist. A smaller player will be able to knock it away. It also will force you to take more time to bring the ball back up if you want to attempt a shot.

Keep the ball high, no lower than chest level and be ready to explode back up the basket. Do not worry about head and shoulder or ball fakes. Go straight back up to the basket before defensive help can arrive. Think — and be — strong. Be prepared to go up, even through contact.

Practice coming down with a missed shot, keep the ball high and going right back to the basket with a follow-up.

## *Tip it with Control*

If you are unable to grab an offensive rebound with both hands and are challenged by an opposing player, try to tip the ball. Depending on your angle and distance from the rim, attempt to tip the ball back to the basket or to an obviously open teammate. By putting the ball back on the rim you might get lucky and the ball may fall in the basket. Even if the ball does not go in the basket, it will allow everyone to battle again for another missed shot.

Do not blindly tip the ball away from the basket. You could be tipping it to the opposition and setting up a fast break opportunity.

Do just the opposite on the defensive end of the court. If you are unable to grab a rebound with both hands and the opposition has a good chance of recovering the rebound, tip the ball away from the basket. Even if the ball goes to an opposing player or out of bounds, your defense will have a chance to reset. If your tip goes to one of your teammates, you may help create a fast break situation.

Practice tip drills with another player boxing you out. Be careful not to go over the other player's back to tip the ball. If you do, you will be called for a foul most every time.

### *Rebounding Free Throws*

Grabbing a defensive rebound on a missed free throw seems pretty routin, but never take it for granted.

If you are occupying a position closest to the basket along the free-throw lane, put your body on the player lined up next to you as soon as the ball begins its downward descent. You have to initiate, then maintain that contact. Keep your body between the basket and your opponent. When the ball hits the rim, go hard for the ball and grab it with both hands.

If you are occupying the second position along the free-throw lane and are watching your teammate shoot a free throw, always assume that the shot will be missed. Be ready to go strong and hard to the basket. The player with inside position will try to put a body on you, but try to avoid the contact by lining up as far away from her as you can in your assigned space. When the ball is headed downward, go hard to the front of the rim for a possible rebound.

Offensive teams may run plays for a second chance opportunity. Instead of making a move to the basket, one of the players can set a screen for the other one, hoping to free up one or both of the players. The players can cut across and form an X. Or they both can spin away from the defenders toward the baseline, hoping for a rebound that shoots sideways.

Defensively, practice blocking out on the free throw lane. Be ready for any special situations that are set up. You have a job to do and boxing out on a free throw is extremely important. Offensively, you want to be a moving target. Practice fighting through or around the block out.

*chapter five*

# Situational Play

## Jump Balls

Even with just one jump ball in games at most levels, do not ignore the situation. The initial jump ball possession can set a tone for the entire game. Overtime periods begin with a jump ball and the first possession of that extra period can be a pivotal one.

Always make certain you know where the safest place is to tap the ball. The key is for your team to gain control of the ball. If you are able to run a play off the jump ball, great, but first make certain a teammate is able to recover the ball.

Simulate a jump ball situation and practice jumping. Practice without a ball and have someone measure how long it takes you to get to your highest point. Adjust the depth of your crouch and the location of your tapping hand to see if that increases your speed. Then practice with a ball. The person who controls the tap is not always the one who jumps the highest, but the one who best times the toss. Experiment with different timings until you have consistency in your speed and height.

## Fast Breaks

Offensive fast break drills already have been discussed. Many times, though, the post player is not part of 2-on-1 or 3-on-2 break. The post player still can get an easy basket as the trailer on a break. How?

When your team has a fast break, the defense is not able to quickly pick up their normal defensive assignments. It is preoccupied with stopping the ball. If you run down the middle of the floor directly to your basket and beat your defender, it is likely that you will be left uncovered. Talk to your teammates and tell them you are trailing. Let them know to look for you. Go hard and look for the ball. If you are not open, take your position at the low post and get into your normal offense.

As you make your dash down the floor, if your defender already is in position in the lane, stop at the free-throw line and look for a pass. Knock down that wide open 15-footer.

Good practice at being the trailer is to enter a normal fast break drill a couple of seconds behind the other offensive players. Do not loaf down to the offensive end of the court. Sprint and you will be surprised how many uncontested baskets you score.

## Loose Balls

It is amazing how confident a team becomes when it begins getting all the loose balls. There is a little bit of luck involved in recovering loose balls. (After all, if the loose balls one night always seem to bounce right into the hands of the opposing team's players, there is not much you can do.) But most loose balls go to the team that is more aggressive and more determined.

Fit that description and chase down every loose ball. Every time your team picks up a loose ball, that is an extra possession. One possession difference can decide a close game.

Practice chasing after loose balls. If it makes you feel more confident, put on a pair of knee and elbow pads or roll out a wrestling mat and practice diving for loose balls. Learn how to tip balls before you go out of bounds. Learn how to scoop up balls while you are on a dead run. It's all about coordination, hustle and determination.

Make it your mind set to get to every loose ball before anyone else.

## Fakes

The best fakes are ones that simulate the start of an actual move.

If you are under the basket and try to fake a shot, you will not fool anyone if you are standing straight up and wave the ball up and down a couple of times. You never would shoot from under the basket just standing there. To shoot, you would bend your knees and begin to rise to the basket. So, if you want to fake out the opposition, your fake should begin with you bending your knees and fake the motion of bringing your body up.

Your eyes are very important. If you are faking a shot, you must visually look to the rim. Make your defender believe you are eyeing up your shot.

If you are out on the floor and want to fake a pass to the right, simulate the pass. If you aren't sure of how you look making a real pass, check a video tape. Then video tape your fakes and compare the actions. See if you would be faked out. Practicing in front of a mirror is another good tool.

Fakes can be a great weapon. They can allow you to shoot unimpeded, throw a pass without any obstacles or drive to the basket on a clear path. Make fakes part of your arsenal.

## Drawing Fouls

Drawing fouls is a skill. No, do not become an award winning actress and begin falling down every time someone gets near you. The officials soon will figure out your shenanigans and never give you the benefit of the doubt.

There are two easy ways to draw fouls. The first is to fake your opponent into the air with a shot fake. If your opponent does not jump up straight, lean into her jumping path and throw up a shot. Chances are good that she will come down on top of you and a foul will be called. If she jumps straight up, do not jump into her path. A good official will recognize that you initiated that contact and is not likely to give you the call.

The second way is to get your opponent on the move. Drive to the basket. Once your opponent is on the move with you, and contact is made, most officials will call a foul on the defender. When a defender is standing flat-footed and has established a position, officials will give the defender the benefit of the doubt when contact is made. However, if both the offensive and defensive players are moving and contact is made, the call usually is against the defender.

Do not attempt to draw a foul every time you have the ball. Use it in key situations when you are trying to get a player her third foul in the first half or her fourth early in the second period or when your opponent is caught off balance.

Practice those moves in a scrimmage before trying them in a game. It is easy to mishandle the ball or to misfire on a shot when you make contact, so make certain you get the call.

## Buzzer Beaters

One-and-seven-tenths seconds remain in the game. Your team has the ball out of bounds under your basket. Is that enough time for you to catch the ball, turn to the basket and shoot a jump shot? What if there were only nine-tenths of a second remaining? Is that long enough? You will never know until you practice.

You should routinely work on getting a shot off before the buzzer sounds. Practice by putting different lengths of time on the clock. Throw the ball in and take a shot. Did you get it off in time? Put a different length of time on the clock and try it again. You may not be able to do anything more than a tip with under five-tenths of a second. Know that in case a game comes down to that.

Also know how long it takes to dribble down the court. If your team has the entire length of the floor to cover with five seconds remaining, do you have to pass the ball the length of the floor on the inbounds pass or does the point guard have time to dribble the ball into the front court? At the end of a game, you want to have the skills needed and the confidence necessary to win the game for your team if you are called upon. Practice a quick release on your shot. You never know when you will need it.

*chapter six*

# Post Drills

## Triangle Shooting

**Purpose:** This is a continuous shooting drill. It enables players to work from every spot on the floor.

**Needed to Execute:** Three players and two balls

**Organization:**

1. Player 1 shoots and follows her shot. After she scores, she passes to player 3 who is calling for the ball.
2. Player 2 takes her shot while player 1 is passing to player 3. Player 1 moves to another area and calls for the ball.
3. Player 2 makes her shot, passes to player 1 and moves to another area, calling for the ball. After player 3 scores, she passes to player 2, etc.

**Coaching Points:**

- Be creative and take shots off the dribble. Post players can also incorporate back to the basket moves.

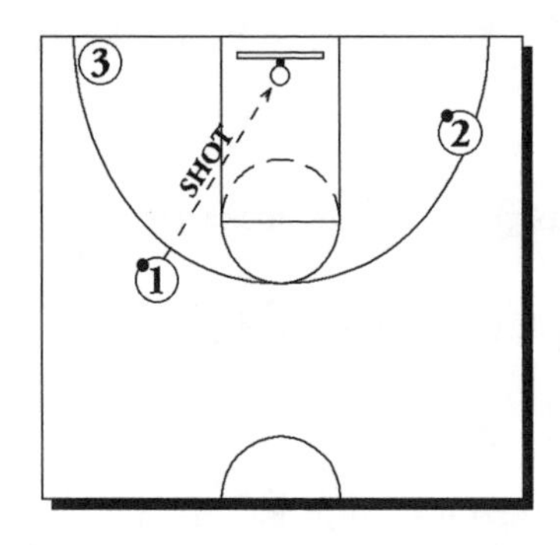


Diagram 1

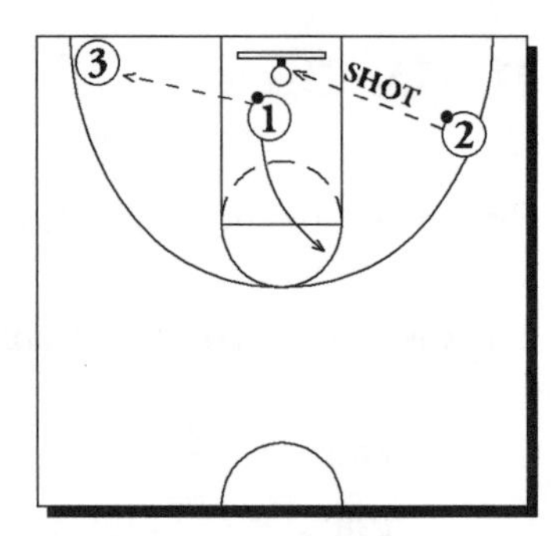


Diagram 2

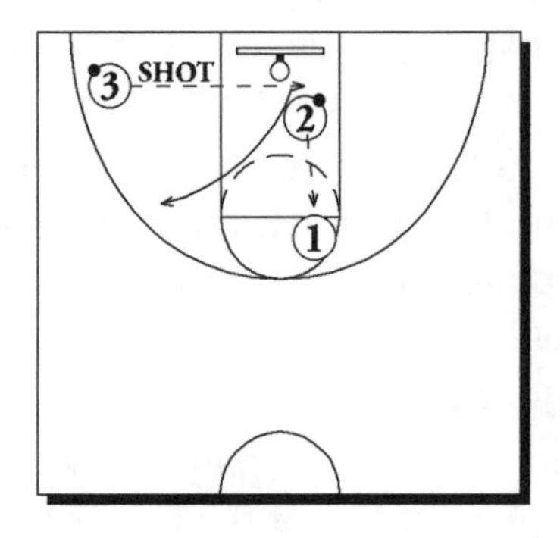


Diagram 3

## 11 Man Break

**Purpose:** This is a continuous 3-on-2 fast break drill.

**Needed to Execute:** Eleven players and one ball

**Organization:**

1. Players 1, 2 and 3 play 3-on-2 offense versus players X1 and X2 (see diagram 1).
2. At the end of the play, the rebounder (any of the five players) outlets the ball to either player 4 or player 5 (see diagram 2).
3. The outlet (4 in the diagram) brings the ball to the middle and, with the rebounder (X2) and the other outlet (5), attacks X3 and X4 in a 3-on-2.

4. At the end of this 3-on-2, the rebounder will outlet to either player 6 or player 7 who will combine to play offense at the opposite end.

5. The correct rotation will have the rebounder becoming offense with the two outlets at the other end. The remaining four players fill in the two defensive spots and the outlet spots.

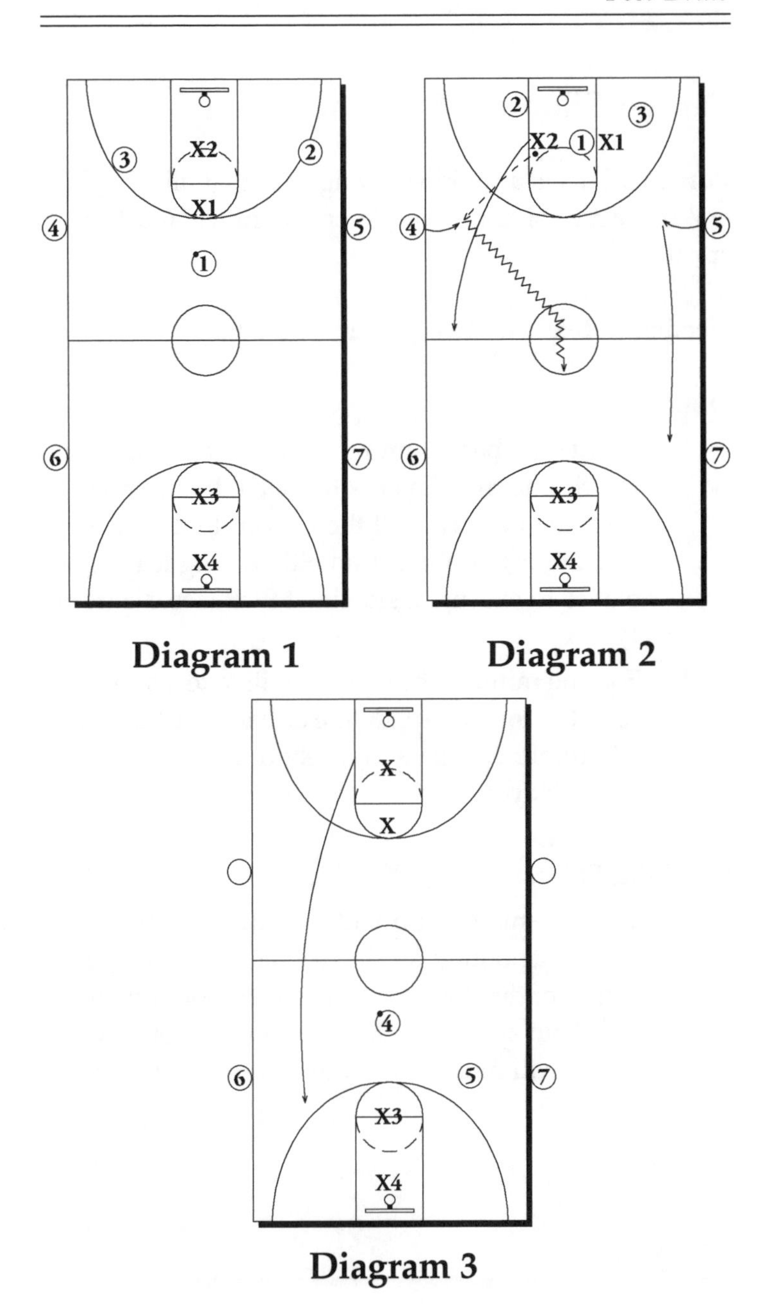


Diagram 1

Diagram 2

Diagram 3

## Partner Shooting/Sideline Touch

**Purpose:** This is a rapid shooting drill that allows players to practice shooting while on the move and from a sprint.

**Needed to Execute:** Two players and a ball

**Organization:**

1. Divide the basket into three areas to determine which line the player is to touch. If she shoots from the top, she will then sprint to the half-court line. Shooting from either wing leads the player to execute a sideline touch (see diagram 1).
2. For one minute, the shooter will take a shot then sprint to touch the sideline or half-court line. The rebounder will pass and rebound during this time. Players then switch roles (see diagram 2).

**Coaching Points:**

- You can mix this up with one-dribble moves to practice shooting off the dribble. Work all areas/angles of the floor. Concentrate on shooting form first. Your sprint should be all out, but before you shoot, you must have body control and balance.

**Diagram 1**

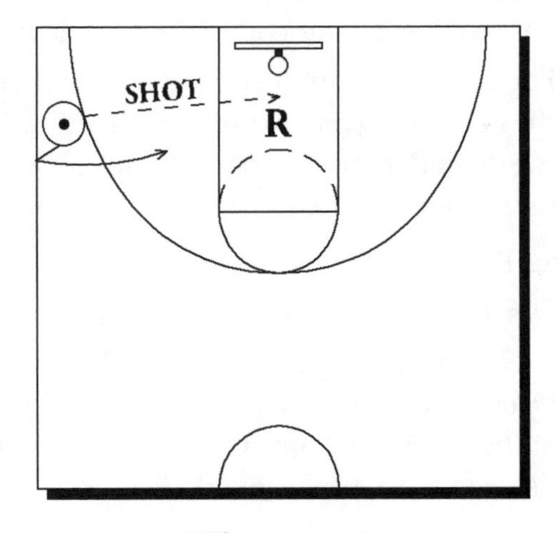


**Diagram 2**

## 3 Man Weave, 2-on-1

**Purpose:** This drill teaches both transition offense and transition defense.

**Needed to Execute:** Three players and a ball

**Organization:**

1. Work a three man "weave" going down the court. Remember the rules to weave are to pass and go behind who you passed to. Do not travel with the ball. Passes are sharp and crisp (see diagram 1).
2. As you approach the free-throw line, the players with the ball jumpstops and makes a bounce pass to the shooter coming in for a layup.
3. For 2-on-1 transition coming back down the court, the passer (player 2) goes back to be the defender. The shooter (3) and player 1 return to play offense (see diagram 2).

**Coaching Points:**

- *Defense:* You want to slow the ball down. Don't let anyone get deeper than you are.
- *Offense:* Advance the ball quickly and go right at the defender. Force the action, before other defensive players recover.

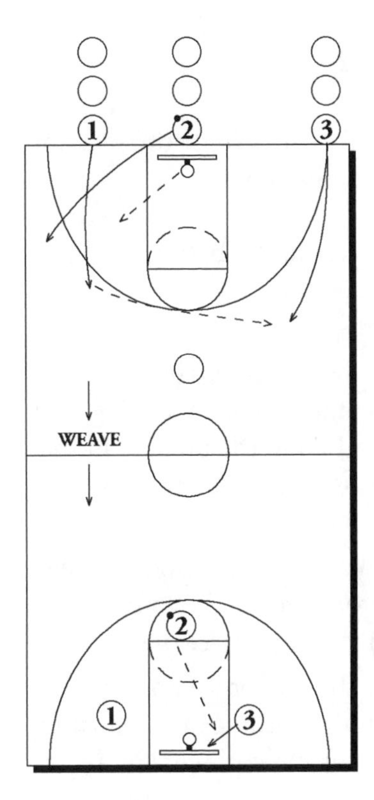


Diagram 1

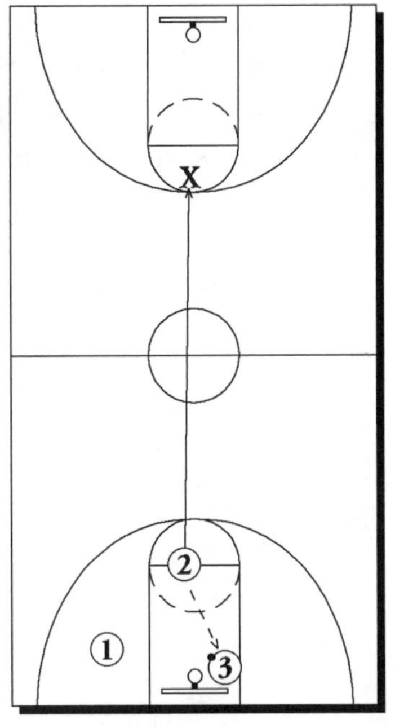


Diagram 2

## 5 Man Weave, 3-on-2

**Purpose:** This transition drill works both offense and defense, as well as passing on the move.

**Needed to Execute:** Five players and a ball

**Organization:**

1. Five players begin at the baseline. They "weave" down the court. Remember when weaving that players are to pass and go to the outside in the direction that they passed (see diagrams 1 and 2).
2. The player that receives near the opposite free throw line (3) jumpstops and makes a bounce pass to the shooter (2) for a layup (see diagram 2).
3. On the return action, the passer (3) and the shooter (2) will touch the endline and return to defend against the other three players in a 3-on-2 (see diagram 3).

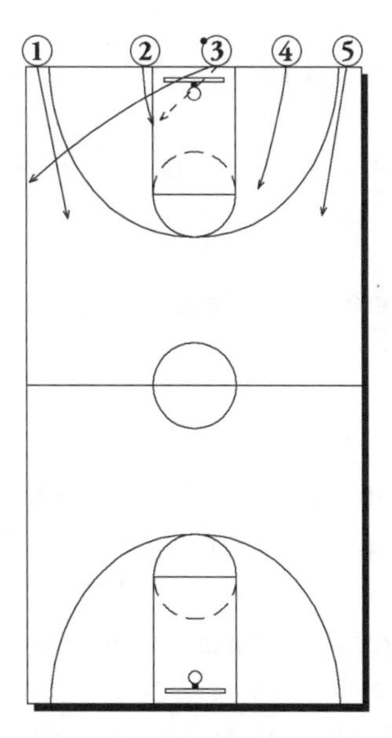


Diagram 1

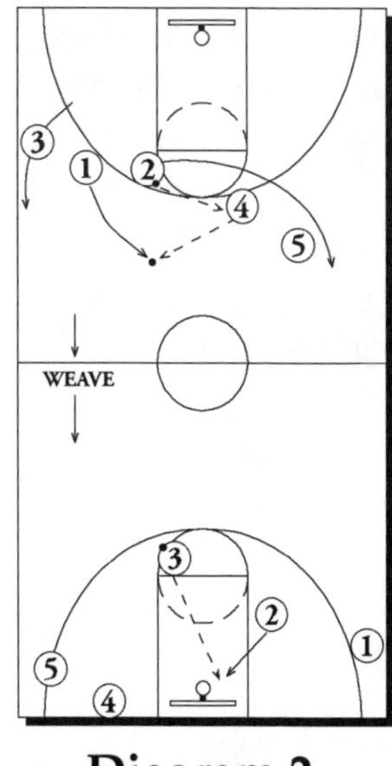


Diagram 2

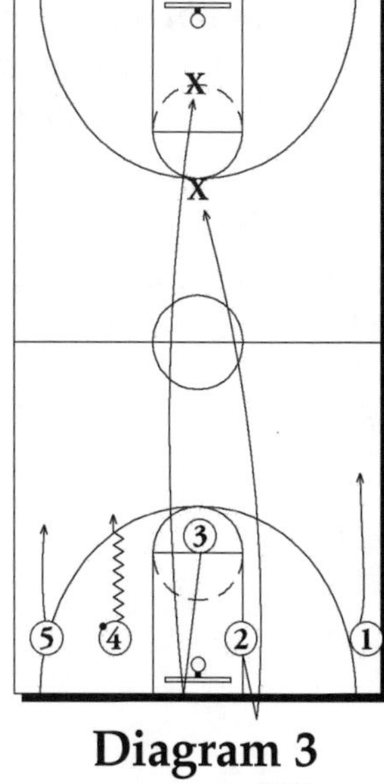


Diagram 3

## Pass and Shoot Drill

**Purpose:** This is a good passing, shooting and conditioning drill.

**Needed to Execute:** Two balls and a minimum of six players

**Organization:**

1. Players line up at both endlines. The first person in each line has a ball. There are four passers (P) positioned as shown in diagram 1.
2. The player (O) passes to the passer (P1) and runs down the sideline. The passer passes back to her. Player O must make the next pass to P2 without traveling. If necessary, she takes one or two dribbles to execute a sharp pass. She then fills the lane wide and angles in to receive the pass back for a shot (see diagram 2).

**Coaching Points:**

- You can vary the shots by using layups, jump shots and moves off the dribble.

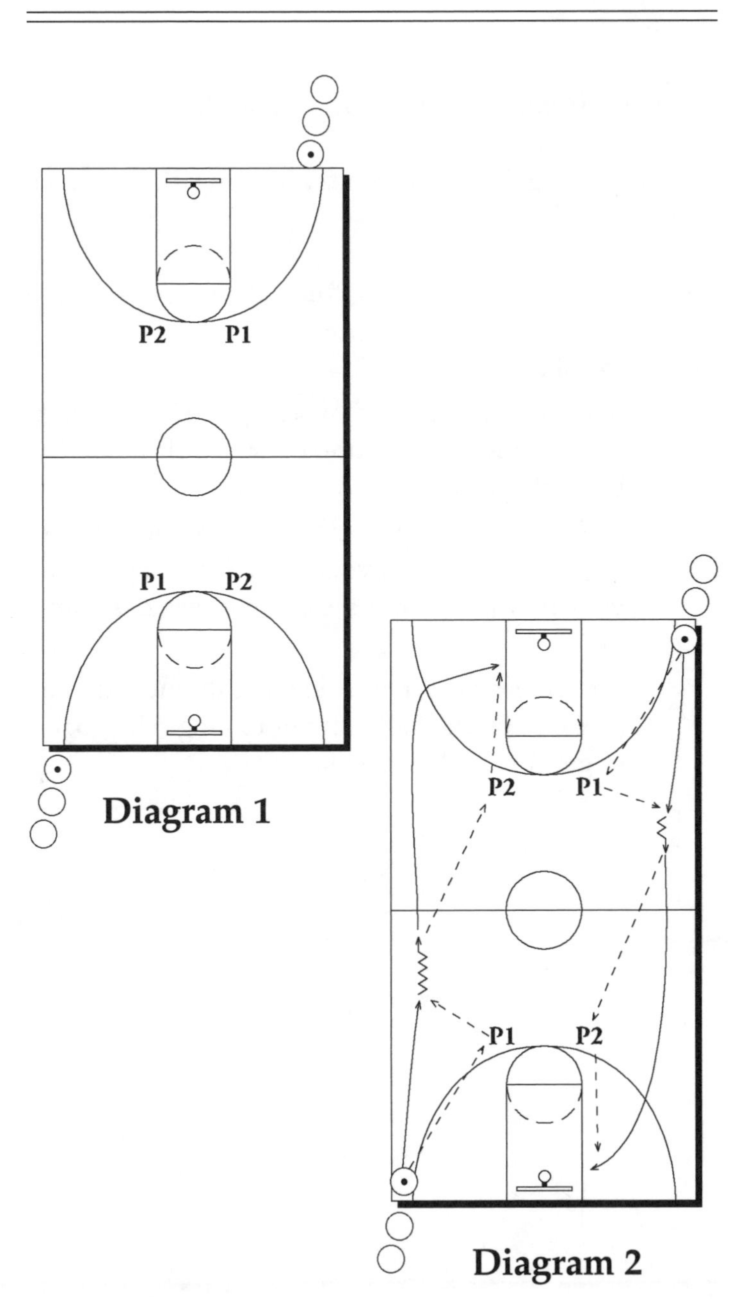


Diagram 1

Diagram 2

## Partner Passing with Defense

**Purpose:** I like this drill to work passing skills versus pressure.

**Needed to Execute:** One ball, three players per group

**Organization:**

1. Start with two players working the basic passes back and forth – bounce, chest, overhead and baseball (see diagram 1).
2. Add a defensive player to pressure the ball. Using well executed pivot and ball fakes, pass to your partner around the defense (see diagram 2).
3. The defensive player is looking to put extreme pressure on the ball without fouling. The goal is to get tips or deflections.

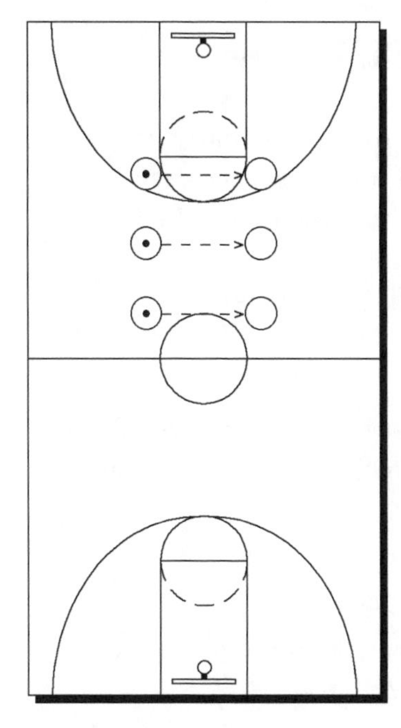

**Diagram 1**

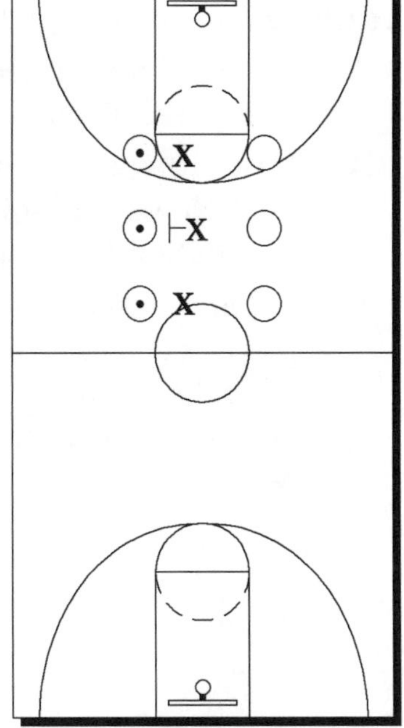


**Diagram 2**

## Passing to the Post with Defense

**Purpose:** This offensive drill works many things. It teaches post players how to hold position against their defense, and it puts game-like pressure on the ball.

**Needed to Execute:** One ball, four players

**Organization:**

The wing player must read the low post defense and make a smart effective pass to her teammate (see diagram 1).

**Coaching Points:** Build on this drill...

- Have the post player make a move and score 1-on-1 (see diagram 2).
- Have the wing defender double down on the post. Now the post is working to make a strong pass out for the wing to shoot (see diagram 3).
- Execute "inside-out-in." Many times a post player's defense will relax when their player kicks the ball out. This is a good time to attack her again (see diagram 4).

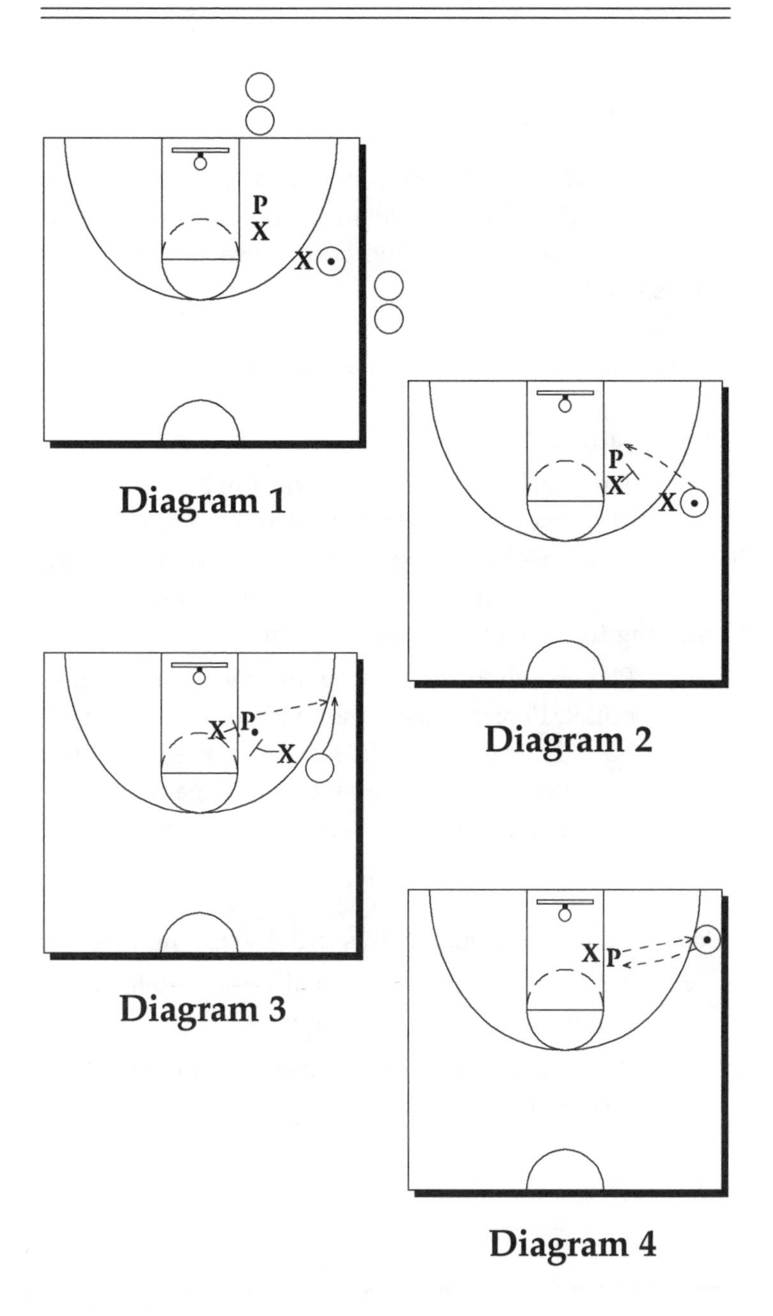


Diagram 1

Diagram 2

Diagram 3

Diagram 4

## Yow Drill

**Purpose:** Named for Coach Kay Yow, who used this drill to lead the 1998 Olympic team to the gold medal, this drill is used for conditioning and to practice transition offense and defense.

**Needed to Execute:** One ball and at least three players

**Organization:**

1. The coach rolls the ball toward halfcourt. The first player in line (1) is looking to pick up that loose ball and go score. The second and third players (2 and 3) are running behind her attempting to distract her (see diagrams 1 and 2).
2. Player 1 shoots the layup and then goes to the outlet. Player 2 takes the made basket out of bounds. Player 3 sprints to touch the baseline and then retreats to play defense against players 1 and 2 coming down to score (see diagram 3).

**Coaching Points:** Build on this drill by adding players.

- Add a fourth player, who also plays defense, making it a 2-on-2 coming back.
- Add a fifth player on offense and simulate 3-on-2 action.

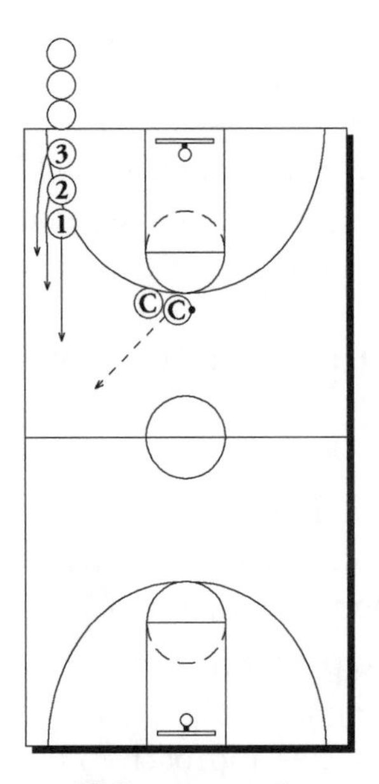


**Diagram 1**

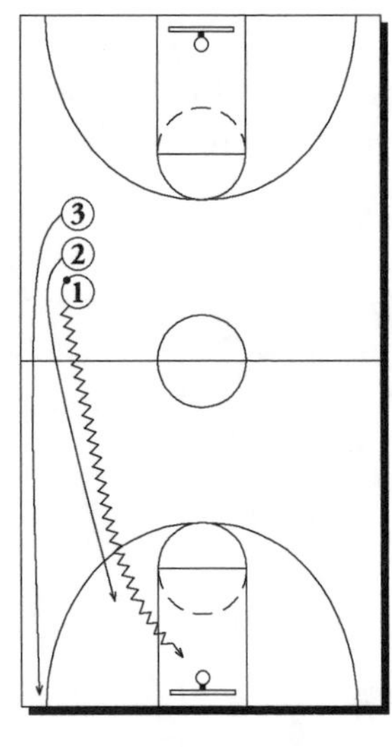


**Diagram 2**

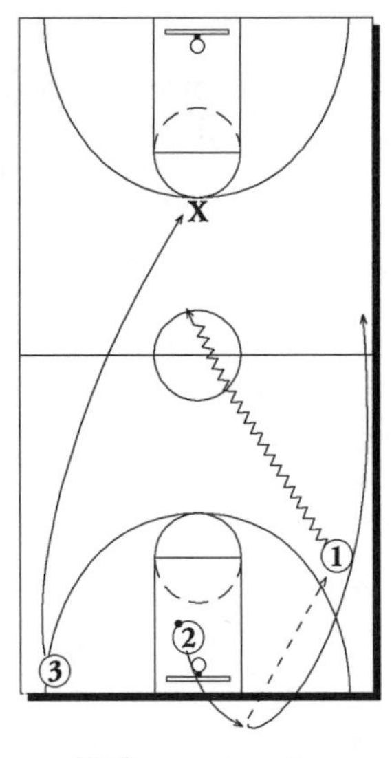


**Diagram 3**

## O-D-O

**Purpose:** I learned this drill from Nell Fortner, coach of the 2000 Olympic gold medal basketball team. This defensive drill works on-ball defense.

**Needed to Execute:** One ball, three players and a passer

**Organization:**

1. Start with a defensive player in the lane and two offensive players wide on the wing, with the rest behind them (see diagram 1).
2. The coach/passer makes a pass to either wing and the defensive player will defend her. She is working on her approach to the ball and then on containing. The offense is trying to score 1-on-1 (see diagram 2).
3. If offense scores, she rotates out. If offense does not score, she becomes the next defensive player.

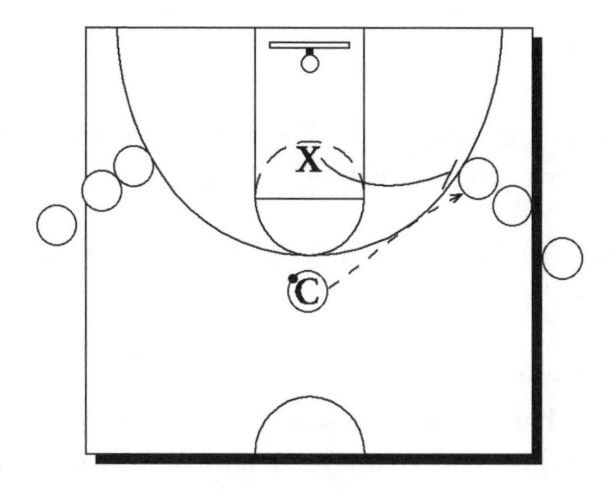


**Diagram 1**

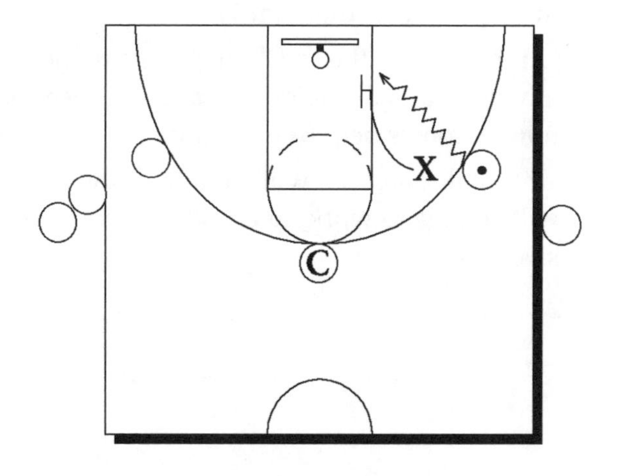


**Diagram 2**

## 2-on-2

**Purpose:** This is a great drill for on-and-off ball defense as well as on-and-off ball rebounding.

**Needed to Execute:** One ball, four players and two passers

**Organization:**

1. There are two passers/coaches up top. At each wing, start an offensive and defensive player.
2. The ballside wing is looking to get open while her defender denies the pass in. The off ball defender is also practicing her defensive concepts in helpside (see diagram 1).
3. On the pass to the coach, the helpside defender advances to ballside denial, and her teammate now becomes help (see diagram 2).
4. Eventually, a coach will shoot and the emphasis will change to working on offensive and defensive rebounding.

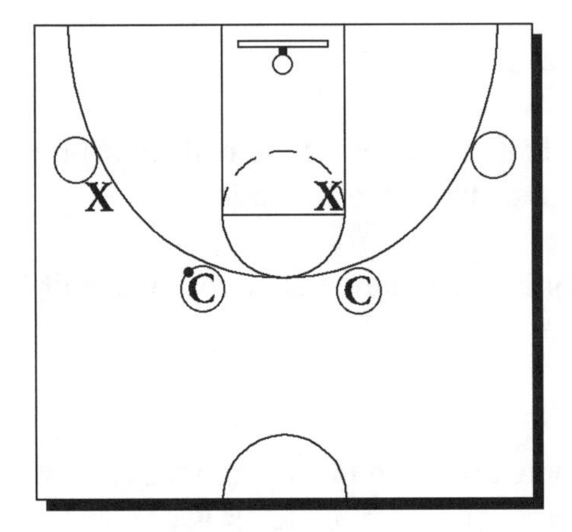


**Diagram 1**

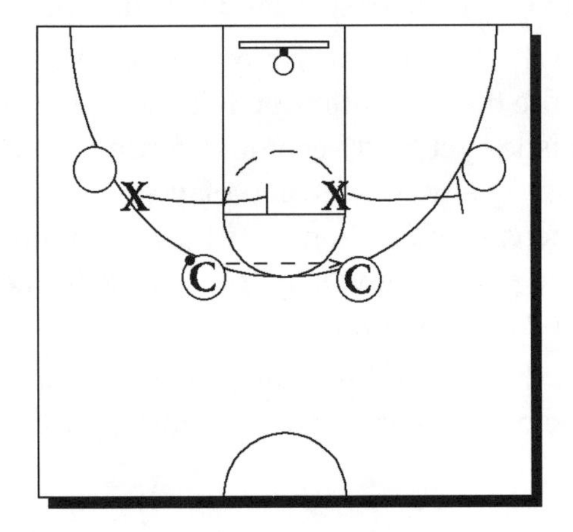


**Diagram 2**

## 3-on-2, 2-on-1

**Purpose:** This is a continuous drill that practices early offensive and defensive transition.

**Needed to Execute:** One ball, a minimum of five players

**Organization:**

1. There are three lines at the baseline with two defenders at opposite ends of court.
2. The three offensive players pass side/counter side until reaching the half court, when they attack the defense 3-on-2 (see diagram 1).
3. At the end of 3-on-2 play, the shooter (if there is more than one attempt, it is the last shooter) will hustle back and become defense on the return trip. The two defensive players now attack offensively for 2-on-1. The 2 remaining offensive players now stay for defense in the next 3-on-2 (see diagram 2).
4. At the end of the 2-on-1, the next 3 players from the baseline are ready to attack 3-on-2.

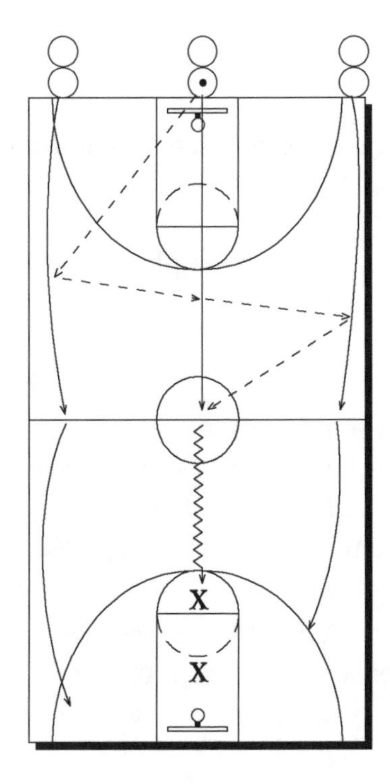


Diagram 1

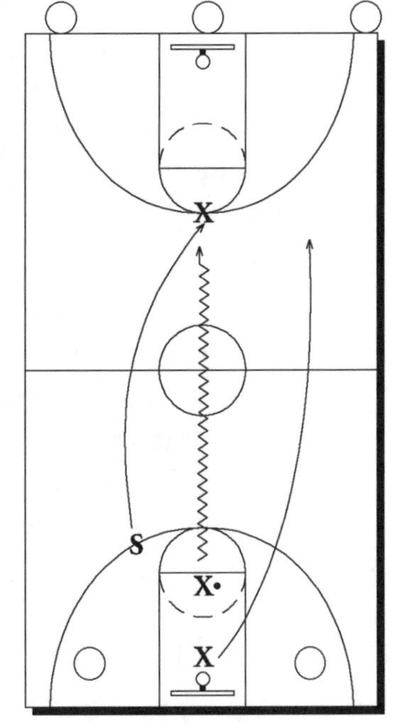


Diagram 2

## Box Out/Outlet Drill

**Purpose:** This drill is to work on boxing out and making a good outlet pass.

**Needed to Execute:** At least two balls, four players and a coach/shooter

**Organization:**

1. There are two lines. The rebounding line is formed on the baseline, and this player will have the ball to give to the coach. The outlet line is a closely formed line behind the coach at the free-throw line (see diagram 1).
2. A coach has the ball at the free-throw line. The rebounder plays defense on the coach by contesting the shot, boxes out and secures the rebound.
3. The outlet player reads where the ball came off and recognizes which side of the floor to look for the outlet (see diagram 2).
4. After the outlet pass is made, the receiver brings the ball to the middle of the floor, while the rebounder fills the lane wide. They advance 2-on-0 to score at the other end.

Diagram 1

Diagram 2

## 2-on-2 Change

**Purpose:** This drill works both offensive and defensive principles. It can be run 2-on-2, 3-on-3, or even 4-on-4 in half court.

**Needed to Execute:** One ball, minimum of four players for 2-on-2, two passers/coaches

**Organization:**

1. Begin with the two lines at half court. You need a passer/coach at the outlet on both sides of the court. The first two players in each line step out to begin the drill.
2. The coach at the outlet has the ball. The two offensive players cut to the basket to receive. Once the ball is passed in, it is a 2-on-2 (see diagrams 1 and 2).
3. At the end of the possession, the ball is outletted to a coach, who called out "change." The offensive players must quickly transition to defense by matching up on the next two players in line. The defense clears. If no "change" is called, defense stays defense on the next two offensive players, and the offense who just played clear the floor.

**Coaching Points:**

- To vary this drill, keep the defense on defense until they stop the offense from scoring, then change.
- Add a third line at half-court and the drill now becomes 3-on-3.

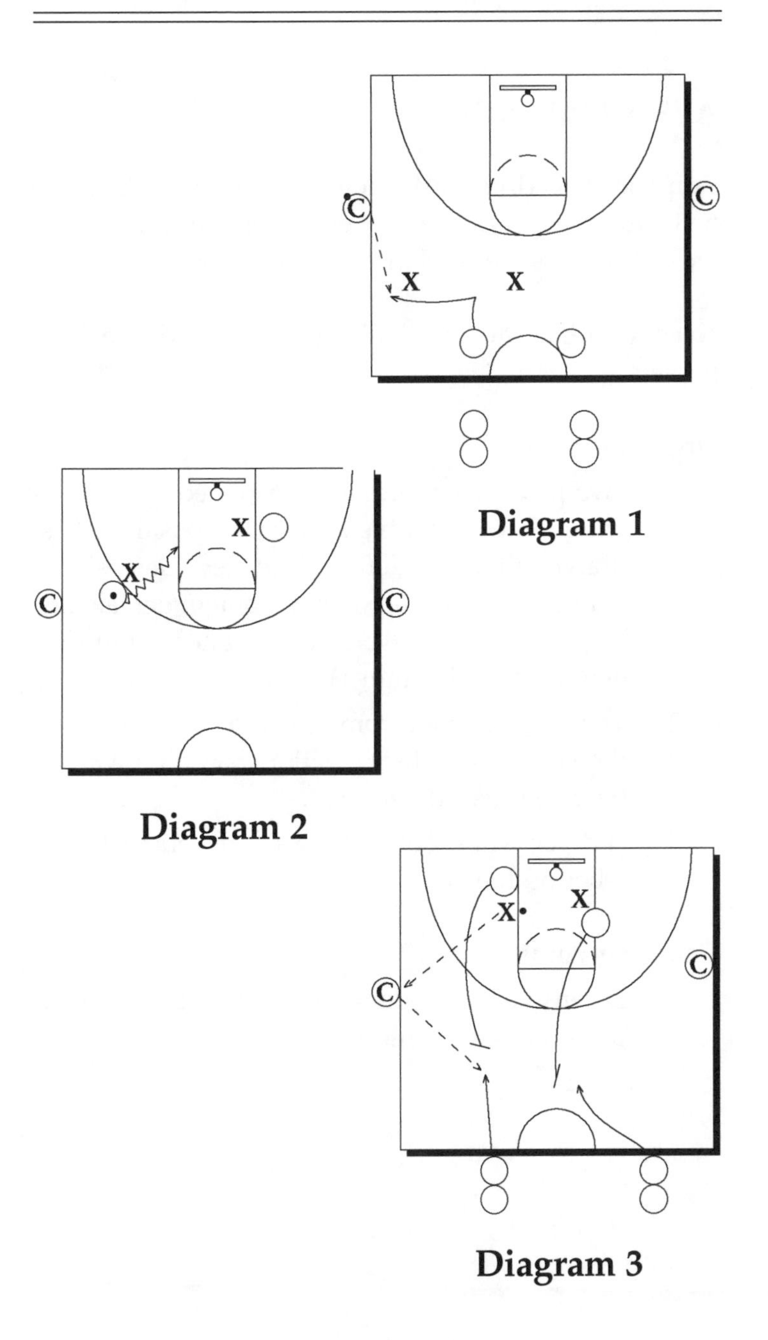


Diagram 1

Diagram 2

Diagram 3

## A Box-Out Drill

**Purpose:** This drill works defensive positioning in the half court as well as boxing out for rebounding. The offensive players are working offensive rebounding.

**Needed to Execute:** One ball, six players, two coaches/passers

**Organization:**

1. Two passers/coaches are positioned at each wing. Three offensive players are positioned as drawn with their defense matched. Defensive players are working on positioning: denial and help. Offensive players are stationery until shot goes up (see diagram 1).
2. The ball is passed from coach to coach and the defense adjusts their position, based on where the ball is (see diagram 2).
3. A coach will shoot and the six players look to rebound the ball.

**Coaching Points:**

- Defensive rebounders must remember to think position first, ball second.

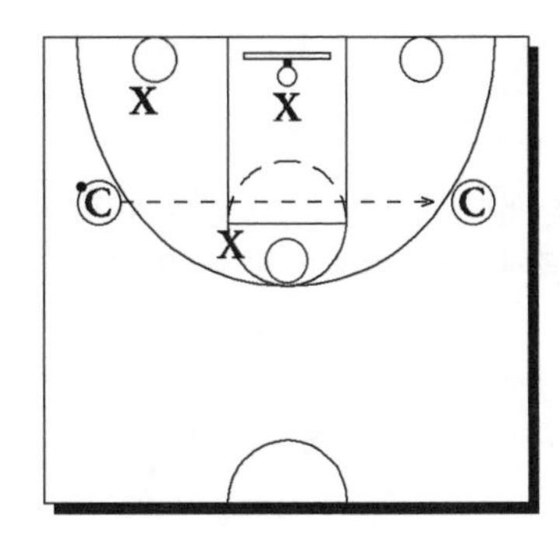


**Diagram 1**

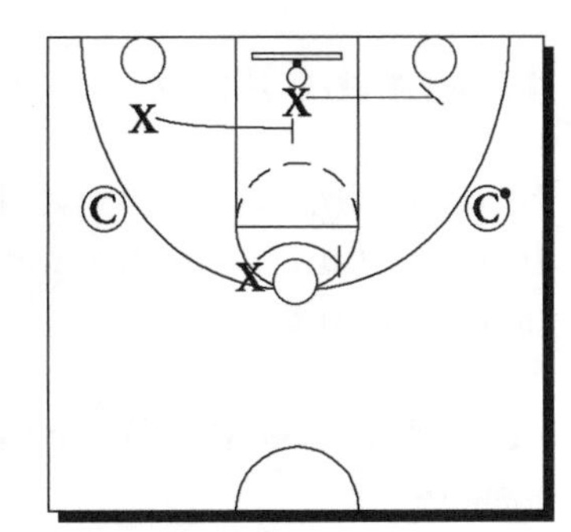


**Diagram 2**

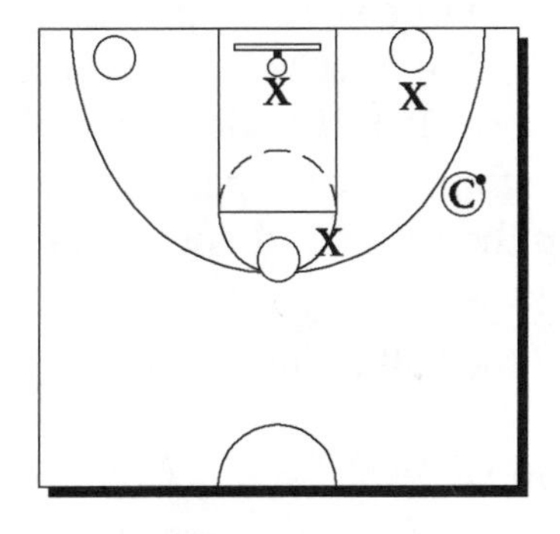


**Diagram 3**

## Bull in the Ring

**Purpose:** This drill is to work post defense. It is a tough drill that builds conditioning, footwork and defensive technique in the post.

**Needed to Execute:** One ball, two players, three or four passers

**Organization:**

1. There are three or four passers around the perimeter. The offensive player looks to cut and post to the ball. The defensive player is moving on the flight of each pass. She is working to bump the cutter and not to let her receive an easy pass.
2. When the ball is entered, it is 1-on-1.

**Coaching Points:**

- This drill is best if started slowly and built on. For example, after each pass make the offensive player hold for a two-second count before cutting to the ball. Gradually you can decrease this time as your post defenders skills increase.
- It is important for the defensive player to realize that the passers have no defense. Therefore, the pass will be entered at some point. Work hard to deny the pass, but when the ball is entered, continue to work to defend your basket.

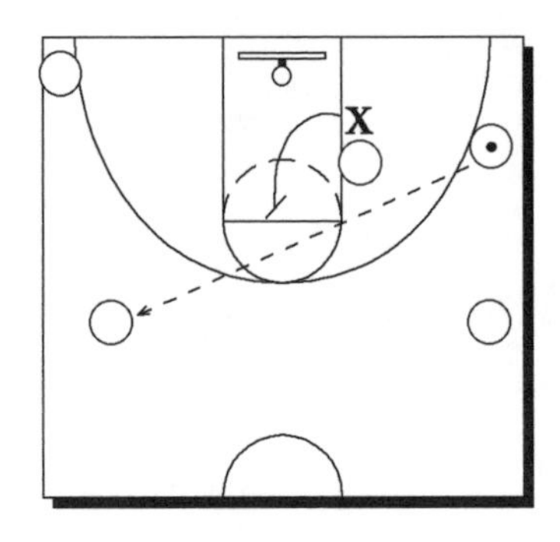


**Diagram 1**

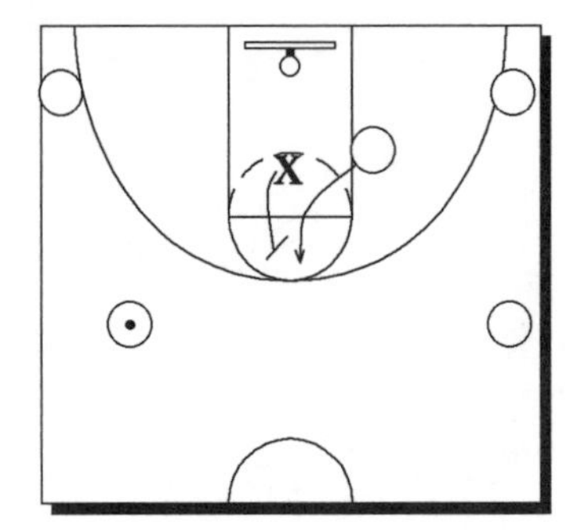


**Diagram 2**

**Diagram 3**